Reading Group Choices

Selections for lively book discussions

2006

Promoting discussible books to reading groups since 1995

W e wish to thank the authors, agents, publicists, and our publishing colleagues who have continued to support this publication by calling to our attention some quality books for group discussion, and the publishers and friends who have helped to underwrite this edition.

Algonquin Books of Chapel Hill

Anchor Books

Ballantine Books

Berkley Books

Calliope Press

Emmis Books

Forge Books

Graywolf Press

Grove/Atlantic

HarperCollins

Haven Books

HCI Books

Henry Holt & Company

Hyperion Books

John Wiley & Sons

Louisiana State University Press

MacAdam/Cage

Middleway Press

MIRA Books

Penguin/Putnam Group

Picador USA

Plume Books

Random House

Red Wheel/Weiser/Conari Press

Riverhead Books

Roots West Press

Southeast Booksellers Association

Soft Skull Press

Thomas Dunne Books

Unbridled Books

Vintage Books

W. W. Norton

Yale University Press

Our heartfelt gratitude also goes to Donna Paz Kaufman and Mark Kaufman of Paz & Associates. Donna and Mark are the founders of *Reading Group Choices* from whom we purchased the business in 2005 and without whose guidance, assistance, and encouragement this edition would not have been possible.

© 2006 *Reading Group Choices*, a division of Connxsys LLC
All Rights Reserved.

Published in the United States by *Reading Group Choices*, a division of Connxsys LLC

ISBN 0-9759742-1-1

For further information, contact:
Barbara Drummond Mead, Publisher
Reading Group Choices
532 Cross Creek Court, Chester, MD 21619 • 410-643-7472
bmead@ReadingGroupChoices.com • www.ReadingGroupChoices.com

Welcome to
Reading Group Choices

"A book is not only a friend, it makes friends for you. When you have possessed a book with mind and spirit, you are enriched. But when you pass it on you are enriched threefold."—Henry Miller

Reading Group Choices 2006 is filled with such enriching friends, just waiting to make new friends for you by passing them on to your reading group. Inside, there is at least one best friend for every group—and many new friends with ideas and experiences that you may not have encountered before. Debut and best-selling authors combine to provide a collection ranging from small-town secrets to thought-provoking dramas to analyses of trends that affect us all. The topics they explore are varied and rich, from the intimacies of relationships and family life to societal change to religious values.

Among its collection, *Reading Group Choices 2006* presents great stories dealing with, of all things, books and reading! *The History of Love* is a tale of irony, imagination, and the grand passions of books and love. *The Jane Austen Book Club* is a sly, witty novel that will thrill Austenites and non-Austenites alike. *Outwitting History* is the fun and true account of Aaron Lansky's adventures gathering abandoned Yiddish books.

Some authors based their novels on the the Vietnam War—*White Ghost Girls* deals with the sacrifice and solidarity of two sisters growing up in Hong Kong during the Vietnam War, and *Carl Melcher Goes to Vietnam* is the simple story of a naive innocent boy sent to fight in 1968.

We have included some fascinating nonfiction titles for you in this edition. *Bait and Switch* is a grim report of the effects of corporate downsizing, and *The Soul of Success* delves into a deeper understanding of success by tapping into women's authentic power. *The Tender Bar* is a captivating, over-the-top funny, yet sad, memoir dealing with a boy without a father who turns to a saloon in search of father figures.

Families, love, divorce, adventure, religion, conflict, secrets, mystery, loss, mental health—all this and more—make for great discussions. Serious and challenging themes and light and breezy reads provide great choices for your reading group year, and *Reading Group Choices 2006* has it all for you! So, invite some new friends (literally and figuratively) to your reading group, and your mind and spirit will be enriched.

—BARBARA AND CHARLIE MEAD

About *Reading Group Choices*

Reading Group Choices' goal is to join with publishers, bookstores, libraries, trade associations, and authors to develop resources to enhance the reading group experience.

Reading Group Choices is distributed annually to bookstores, libraries, and directly to book groups. Titles from previous issues are posted on the **www.ReadingGroupChoices.com** website. Books presented here have been recommended by book group members, librarians, booksellers, literary agents, publicists, authors, and publishers. All submissions are then reviewed to ensure the discussibility of each title. Once a title is approved for inclusion by the Advisory Board (see below), publishers are then asked to underwrite production costs, so that copies of *Reading Group Choices* can be distributed for a minimal charge.

For additional copies, please call your local library or bookstore, or contact us by phone or email as shown below. Quantities are limited. For more information, please visit our website at **www.ReadingGroupChoices.com**

410-643-7472 • info@ReadingGroupChoices.com

READING GROUP CHOICES ADVISORY BOARD

Donna Paz Kaufman founded the bookstore training and consulting group of Paz & Associates in 1992, with the objective of creating products and services to help independent bookstores and public libraries remain viable in today's market. A few years later, she met and married **Mark Kaufman**, whose background included project management, marketing communications, and human resources. Together, they launched *Reading Group Choices* in 1995 to bring publishers, booksellers, libraries, and readers closer together. They now offer training and education for new and prospective booksellers, architectural design services for bookstores and libraries, marketing support through *The Reader's Edge* customer newsletter, and some print and video products on a wide variety of topics. To learn more about Paz & Associates, visit www.pazbookbiz.com.

John Mutter is editor-in-chief of *Shelf Awareness*, the daily e-mail newsletter focusing on books, media about books, retailing, and related issues to help booksellers, librarians, and others do their jobs more effectively. Before he and his business partner, Jenn Risko, founded the company in May 2005, he was executive editor of bookselling at *Publishers Weekly*, where among many other duties, he founded the old *PW Daily for Booksellers*, the first daily e-mail newsletter in the industry. He has covered book industry issues for 25 years and written for a variety of publications, including *The Bookseller* in the U.K., *Australian Bookseller & Publisher*, and *Boersenblatt*, the German book trade magazine. For more information about *Shelf Awareness*, go to its website, www.shelf-awareness.com.

Mark Nichols was an independent bookseller in various locations from Maine to Connecticut from 1976 through 1993. After seven years in a variety of positions with major publishers in New York and San Francisco, he joined the American Booksellers Association in 2000, and currently serves as the Director of Book Sense Marketing. He is also on the Board of the Small Press Center, and has edited two volumes with Newmarket Press —*Book Sense Best Books* (2004) and *Book Sense Best Children's Books* (2005).

CONTENTS

 On page 7, read how you can win a discussion with an author!

Look for this icon and **your reading group** could be a

WINNER!

When this icon is displayed with a book's Topics for Discussion, it indicates that the author is available by phone to answer reading groups' questions.

Did you ever want to ask an author how a character was created?

Or ask whether an author is planning to write a sequel?

MAYBE YOU CAN!

All you have to do is REGISTER and WIN!

To win an opportunity for your reading group to have a lively discussion with an author, please register at
www.ReadingGroupChoices.com

Contests begin in December 2005.
Author/group discussions will be scheduled for 2006.

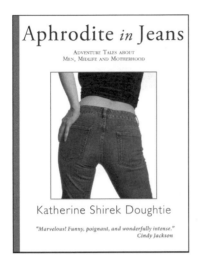

Aphrodite *in* Jeans

ADVENTURE TALES ABOUT
MEN, MIDLIFE AND MOTHERHOOD

Katherine Shirek Doughtie

"Marvelous! Funny, poignant, and wonderfully intense."
Cindy Jackson

APHRODITE IN JEANS
Adventure Tales about Men, Midlife and Motherhood

Author: *Katherine Shirek Doughtie*

Publisher: Haven Books, 2005

Website: www.aphroditeinjeans.com

Available in:
Paperback, 256 pages, $13.95
ISBN 978-1-58436-800-7

Subject: Relationships/Women/
Memoir (Nonfiction)

Summary: In *Aphrodite in Jeans*, Katherine Shirek Doughtie explores what happens when a woman stalemated in the middle of life dares to answer a call to live more fully. Whether discussing motherhood, working through relationships or taking care of an aging parent, these essays are in turn funny, poignant and challenging. With wicked insight and unflinching courage, Ms. Doughtie ruthlessly examines her experiences as she dares to tackle life head on.

Katherine Shirek Doughtie holds degrees in Creative Writing/Literature from the University of California, Santa Cruz and an MFA from UCLA in Motion Picture/Film, Screenwriting. She has written audio dramatizations for the Louis L'Amour Audio Books series, sold several screenplays and written essays and articles for print and online magazines. This is her first published collection of essays.

Topics for Discussion

1. In this book, the author talks about a "call to adventure" in midlife, prompting her to make significant life changes. How would you live your life if you knew you had one year left? Five years left? Ten? Given that you don't know whether you have five minutes or fifty years left, how is that different from how you currently live your life?

2. In the beginning of the book, the author meets someone who changes her life. Who in your life challenges you to change or grow? Does what someone stands for, or how they live their life, sometimes force you to look at your own life in a different way?

3. In "Love Before First Sight," the author describes online romances. Have you ever flirted with someone via email? Were you more (or less) honest with that person because of the safety of email? If you wrote before you met in person, how did "reality" differ from what you had imagined?

4. Describe the "ideal" you, in terms of physical appearance. To what lengths would you go to get to that ideal? What benefit(s) would you get by looking like that? Would it be worth it?

5. In "The Delicate Art of Lying" the author talks about lying by being honest. Do you consider omitting part of the truth a true lie? Can you tell when someone is lying to you? How? Do you want your partner to be really honest with you, even if it would hurt your feelings?

6. What is your checklist in looking for a potential mate? Of the good relationships you've had in your life, how many matched up to that checklist? Do you think what you want and what you need are two different things?

7. The media implies that younger bodies are attractive and more beautiful than older ones. However, in "The Aphrodite Phase" the author describes an increased comfort, freedom and acceptance as she grows older. Where does beauty and attractiveness come from? Does it come from physical attributes or mental attitude? Were you happier in your skin when you were younger? Or have you grown more comfortable as you've aged?

8. The title "Aphrodite in Jeans" refers to a contemporary, down-to-earth version of the Greek goddess of love and sexuality. If Aphrodite were your roommate, what would you want to ask her? What would she teach you about yourself? How would she challenge you to live?

BAIT AND SWITCH
The (Futile) Pursuit of the American Dream

Author: *Barbara Ehrenreich*

Publisher: Metropolitan Books, 2005

Website: www.henryholt.com
www.barbaraehrenreich.com

Available in:
Hardcover, 256 pages. $24.00
ISBN 0-8050-7606-9

Subject: Current Affairs (Nonfiction)

Subject: In 1998, journalist Barbara Ehrenreich became a waitress, a maid, and a low level sales clerk while researching *Nickel and Dimed: On (Not) Getting By in America*. Selling close to one million copies, *Nickel and Dimed* exposed the truth about the demise of a living wage, health insurance, and other presumed rewards for American workers. In *Bait and Switch: The (Futile) Pursuit of the American Dream*, she goes undercover once again, this time to explore the grim results of corporate downsizing. Immersed in the world of the white-collar unemployed, she joins the ranks of those who seem to have done everything right—finished college, gained professional experience, honed an impressive resume—yet cannot land a steady job in corporate America. Written with hilarious candor, impeccable research, and clear-eyed respect for the faces behind the statistics, *Bait and Switch* exposes the untold cruelties of today's economy.

Barbara Ehrenreich is the author of thirteen books, including the *New York Times* bestsellers *Nickel and Dimed* and *The Worst Years of Our Lives*, as well as *Blood Rites* and *Fear of Falling*, which was nominated for a National Book Critics Circle Award. A frequent contributor to *Harper's Magazine* and *The Nation*, she has been a columnist for *The New York Times* and *Time*. She lives in Virginia.

Topics for Discussion

1. Discuss your own career path. How has corporate downsizing, reorganizing or outsourcing affected your life?

2. Ehrenreich recalls her father's experience climbing the corporate ladder in the 50s and 60s. He was loyal to his company, and it in turn was loyal to him. Would this be a reasonable expectation today? How have corporations changed in the way they treat their employees over the last generation?

3. Throughout her job search, Ehrenreich is struck by the constant advice to adopt a "positive attitude" no matter what you're going through as an unemployed person. Do you think this is a good psychological strategy? Or do we pay a price for constantly concealing anger and sadness under a happy face?

4. In chapter three, "Surviving Boot Camp," Ehrenreich's coach insists that we only have ourselves to blame for whatever happens to us in life. How widespread do you think this idea is in our culture? Would you call it "victim blaming" or a correct assessment of one's personal responsibility? What do you think is the effect of this idea on people struggling with unemployment?

5. Chapter five, "Networking with the Lord," describes the evangelical Christian groups Ehrenreich stumbled onto in her quest for employment. Was she right to be critical of their proselytizing? What role, if any, should religion play in a secular workplace?

6. Discuss the gender and racial dimensions of job searching. Do you think Ehrenreich's experience would have been different if she had been male, or a person of color?

7. Discuss the book's title. What are college-educated young Americans being lured into? If a college education—even in a business major—no longer offers occupational security, how should young people think about their careers?

8. What were your thoughts as you finished reading *Bait and Switch*? Is there any action you can take to reverse the trend toward greater job insecurity? Do you predict that legislation will ever be passed limiting a corporation's ability to lay people off at will or outsource jobs overseas? Can the compensation gap between CEOs and other employees keep expanding indefinitely?

For additional discussion topics for Bait & Switch, *visit www.henryholt.com*

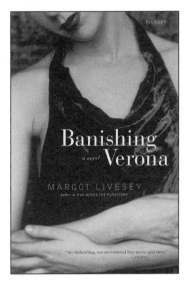

BANISHING VERONA

Author: *Margot Livesey*

Publisher: Picador USA, 2005

Website: www.picadorusa.com

Available in:
Paperback, 353 pages. $14.00
ISBN 0-312-42520-1

Subject: Relationships/
Women's Fiction (Fiction)

Summary: Zeke is twenty-nine, a man who looks like a Raphael angel and who earns his living as a painter and carpenter in London. He reads the world a little differently from most people and has trouble with such ordinary activities as lying, deciphering expressions, recognizing faces. Verona is thirty-seven, confident, hot-tempered, a modestly successful radio-show host, unmarried, and seven months pregnant. When the two meet in a house that Zeke is renovating, they fall in love, only to be separated less than twenty-four hours later when Verona mysteriously disappears.

Both Zeke and Verona, it turns out, have complications in their lives, though not of a romantic kind. Verona's involve her brother, Henry, who is embroiled in shady financial dealings. Zeke's father has had a heart attack, and his mother is threatening to run away with her lover. And yet, knowing as little as he does about her, Zeke is consumed only with finding Verona.

"[Livesey's] great gift is for concrete, tactile detail. Characters' appearances are rendered with startling vividness. . . . And Livesey has a wonderful way with evocations of atmosphere and states of mind."
—**Katherine Dieckmann,** *The New York Times Book Review*

Margot Livesey is the award-winning author of a story collection, *Learning by Heart,* and of the novels *Homework, Criminals, The Missing World,* and *Eva Moves the Furniture,* which was a *New York Times* Notable Book, an *Atlantic Monthly* Best Book of the Year, and a PEN/Winship finalist. Born in Scotland, she currently lives in the Boston area, where she is writer in residence at Emerson College.

Topics for Discussion

1. What makes Verona flee after the first night she spends with Zeke? Why does she nail her clothes to the floor? How does Zeke understand this gesture?

2. Zeke often feels ill at ease with other people yet in less than forty-eight hours he falls in love with Verona. Why does he respond to her so strongly?

3. How does Zeke function in the world? Why is restoring antique clocks the perfect hobby for him and why does he think that the clocks amplify his spirit? Zeke tells a nurse that his feelings stay constant as cathedrals. Is this true? What caused his breakdown?

4. What sort of a man is Henry? How does he rationalize what he does with his grandfather's will? Verona says she and Henry share the same corrupt moral gene. Do you agree? Why does Verona feel such a sense of responsibility to Henry when he clearly thinks only about himself?

5. What is Henry's attitude to money? How does this affect his relationship with his sister, his best friend and the woman he hopes to marry?

6. Zeke believes that his mother regards him as "broken beyond fixing." Is this really how Gwen sees him? To what extent does her behavior exacerbate his difficulties? What is the nature of Zeke's disorder? Does the novel suggest that his difficulties also have their rewards?

7. Zeke is described as looking like a Raphael angel and Henry is referred to as beautiful. How do these two very different men relate to their appearance? What else do they have in common that attracts Verona to Zeke?

8. What makes Zeke decide to tell his father about his mother's infidelity? Was this the right choice?

9. Would Jill and Zeke have become friends if they had met in London? What do they have in common besides being visitors to a foreign country?

10. Near the end of the novel Verona tells Zeke about a princess who is immune to gravity except when she swims in the palace lake. What does Verona hope to suggest by telling this story?

11. What does the title *Banishing Verona* refer to? What does Zeke mean at the end of the novel when he says that he'll 'try'? Is there a future for Zeke and Verona?

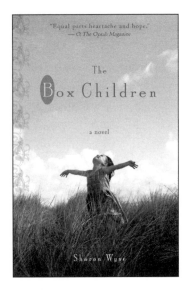

THE BOX CHILDREN

Author: *Sharon Wyse*

Publisher: Riverhead Books, 2002

Websites: www.theboxchildren.com
www.penguinputnam.com

Available in:
Paperback, 183 pages. $13.00
ISBN 1-57322-996-2

Subject: Hope/Family Strife/Survival
(Fiction)

Summary: "I can put my eyes just at the top of the wheat and see the world stretch out flat to the sky." With this secret diary entry, a lonely girl on a Texas wheat farm sets her sights on the larger life she yearns for. Her only companions are the Box Children, five tiny dolls she endows with the lives they lost as her mother's miscarried babies over the years. With no privacy at all, a brave and clear-eyed Lou Ann Campbell writes her way through a coming-of-age summer as her mother's latest pregnancy brings increasing insanity to the season's harvest. Filled with honesty, humor, and romance, *The Box Children* will leave its mark on your heart.

"A trenchant debut novel that is equal parts heartache and hope."
—O, The Oprah Magazine

"Wry and heartfelt, this is a quietly impressive debut. Bottom Line: Open this Box." —People

"This powerful story of adaptation and survival is recommended for all fiction collections." —Library Journal

"The Box Children *is an amazing tale that will speak to readers everywhere." —*Mickey Pearlman, *What to Read*

Sharon Wyse is a native Texan who spent her summers on a wheat farm until she was fifteen. *The Box Children*, her first novel, was a finalist for the 2003 Violet Crown Book Award. She lives in Brooklyn, New York.

Topics for Discussion

1. One aspect of coming of age literature is a new awareness of self as separate from family. How does this dawn on Lou Ann? How did it dawn on you?

2. Lou Ann has a strong moral and ethical sense, distinct from the strict rules and taboos she is raised with. Is this common? Do you have memories of your own moral awareness as a child, separate from what your parents may have taught?

3. Miscarriages are a huge area of non-public grieving and great distress, loss, and shame. Loretta Campbell's life has been misshapen by this experience. Has the situation changed since the 1960s? What's different about suffering that is and isn't talked about?

4. It could be said that Lou Ann belongs to Mother, and Will belongs to Daddy. There's also the separation of women/inside and men/outside. What did each gender lose from this situation? How did Lou Ann try to break out of these barriers?

5. When Lou Ann reads magazines, it's the ads she really takes in, that affect her understanding of what life offers. Is this true for children today? Grownups?

6. Were you worried about what Earl might do? Why wasn't Lou Ann?

7. What makes Mother both likeable and hateable? What lets Daddy off the hook or condemns him?

8. Young people cobble together a universe that has what they need in it. What needs of Lou Ann's are met by writing? By the Box Children? By Alva Higgins and Wyn Rue? By Earl and Lonnie? By her mother, father, and brother?

9. Lou Ann's family looks "perfect" from the outside—in fact, other mothers send their babies to Loretta for care and training. Lou Ann describes situations that outsiders don't see, until the trouble breaks out into the open. Is it harder for children if things fall apart or if they don't?

10. The year was 1960, but in rural America much was the same as it had been for the past 30 years. How much of a time/reality/values schism still exists between rural and urban parts of the country?

Other reading guides are available at www.penguin.com/guides
and www.readinggroupguides.com

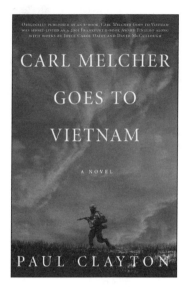

CARL MELCHER GOES TO VIETNAM

Author: *Paul Clayton*

Publisher: Thomas Dunne Books/ St. Martin's Press, 2004

Website: www.carlmelcher.com

Available in:
Hardcover, 197 pages. $21.95
ISBN 0-312-32903-2

Subject: War/Vietnamese Conflict/ African American Soldiers/ Race Relations (Fiction)

Summary: The year is 1968. Like thousands of other American boys, Carl Melcher is drafted and sent to Vietnam. His new company is infected with the same racial tensions plaguing the nation. Despite that, Carl makes friends on both sides of the color line. The war, like a tiger lurking in the bushes, picks off its victims one by one. Naively over-optimistic, Carl believes that karma and good intentions will save him and his friends. Then fate intervenes to teach Carl something of the meaning of life, and death.

"In this fictional account of the Vietnam War, Clayton shuns drama and political issues, detailing instead the minutiae of one soldier's experience. The simple language reflects the identity of an uncertain youth drawn involuntarily into a new and unfamiliar world. . . . This novel does reveal Clayton, himself drafted in 1968, to be a reflective and strategic writer."
—Library Journal

Paul Clayton was drafted in 1968 and sent to Vietnam in September of that year. Clayton served with an infantry line company in the Central Highlands of Pleiku Province. After the army, he received a BA in English Literature from Temple University. He is the author of *Calling Crow*, *Flight of the Crow*, and *Calling Crow Nation*. *Carl Melcher Goes to Vietnam* was a finalist at the 2001 Frankfurt eBook Awards for nonfiction. Paul Clayton currently lives and works in California.

Topics for Discussion

1. Distracted by his emotional pain and his immature fantasies, Carl's mind is not on his job, and one could argue that he is not a very effective soldier. In fact, Carl even (jokingly?) suggests that the war is not real. Would more training have made Carl a better soldier? And what form would that training take—physical, emotional, or mental?

2. Discuss the two alpha males in the squad, Ron and Glock. What are their attitudes about life and the war in Vietnam, and how were they formed? And whose attitude, Ron's or Glock's, prevails in the squad, and why?

3. There was much debate in America over the war in Vietnam. Where in the novel is that addressed?

4. Discuss Mike's death by friendly fire. Whose fault was it? Can these things ever be eliminated?

5. Discuss the death of the PAVN medic. Was there anything unusual about this action? What does this scene reveal about the characters?

6. Carl Melcher had a very sketchy understanding of Buddhism. Do you think this was a help or a hindrance to him? Is religious belief a help or a hindrance to those waging war?

7. Discuss the final scenes in the hospital and Carl's friendship with Greg Mills and Jack Krouse. The most troubled character here seems to be Krouse; the most balanced, Mills. Carl seems to be somewhere in between. With which character did you most identify? Why?

8. What has Carl learned by the end of the novel? Are these "lessons" true only in relation to the Vietnam war, or do they apply to all wars?

9. How much of the book do you think is autobiographical?

10. "War is hell," the saying goes, and much has been written about the behavior of young men during war. Based on your reading of the novel and your discussions with others, what do you think about the morality and behavior of *these* American soldiers in comparison with the soldiers of other nations?

11. The majority of soldiers in the field during the Vietnam War were draftees. Career soldiers and National Guard units are fighting the current war in Iraq and Afghanistan. Which do you think is more effective, and why? Do you think the draft will ever be re-instated?

THE DESERT DWELLERS TRILOGY

Author: *Harriet Rochlin*

Publisher: Roots West Press, 2004

Website: www. rochlin-roots-west. com

Available in:
Paperback, $28.00
ISBN 0-9741349-6-1

Subject: Women/Western/Jewish (Fiction)

Summary: This packaged set of three acclaimed novels, covers twelve transformative years—1875 to 1887—in the life of the series' big-hearted protagonist. *The Reformer's Apprentice* opens with Frieda juggling a double life: adoring follower of a pioneer feminist and unpaid, harassed cook at her father's San Francisco kosher boardinghouse. At twenty-two, she flees with an Arizona pioneer, a Jew, of sorts. In the *First Lady of Dos Cacahuates* Frieda survives sandstorms, flashfloods, heat, infidelity (surprisingly hers), fraudulence, and poverty. But Bennie's love for her, Dos Cacahuates, and the desert proves contagious. Reckoning occurs in *On Her Way Home*, when her visiting kid sister is kidnapped by a murderer. Obsessed with reclaiming the girl, Frieda, on her own, pits herself against Arizona's crude justice system in three jails, two boisterous courtrooms, and at a bizarre execution. She emerges mangled, but sure of where she is, and with whom she belongs.

"The author serves up enough period charm, crackling storytelling, and priceless details to satisfy devotees of both wild west lore and Jewish history." —Publishers Weekly

Harriet Rochlin, a native of Los Angeles, has been researching and writing on Jewish roots in the Spanish, Mexican and American West for more than three decades. Her landmark social history, *Pioneer Jews: A New Life in the Far West*, is now in its eleventh printing. She turned to fiction to probe the inner lives of these pioneers as they progressed from newcomers to westerners. A recognized authority on western Jewish history in fact and fiction, Rochlin lectures nationwide.

Topics for Discussion

1. What does the author hope to convey with the title Desert Dwellers Trilogy, and by references throughout the series to the transformative powers of the wilderness?

2. How do the lives of Jews pioneering in increasingly urban California contrast with those of Jews in the Arizona Territory?

3. In what ways does the trilogy differ from a traditional Western? An American Jewish immigrant story? A female Bildungsroman?

4. Contrast Frieda's behavior among the Sisters of Service, at Levie's Kosher Boardinghouse, as Frieda Levie Goldson in Dos Cacahuates? Frieda on her own in the Arizona Territory?

5. Did Bennie's harrowing frontier experiences explain his ability to accept setbacks and move on? If so, what in Frieda's earlier years induce her to join him in pioneering?

6. An actual 1886 family murder and kidnapping in the Arizona Territory inspired the third novel. Why did the author choose to involve her characters in a calamity of this nature?

7. Were the Levies thinking of their own or of Ida's reputation when they insisted she stay in Dos Cacahuates until outward evidence of her tragic experience had vanished?

8. How do you interpret Frieda's method of extracting a confession from the murderer? What did she learn interacting at close range with a man who had inflicted life-altering pain on her and her loved ones?

9. The characters in these tragi-comic novels are portrayed as complex human beings, alternately loving, dismissive, optimistic, dubious, elated, depressed, funny, grim, altruistic, self-centered. Is the author depicting a particular time, place, and circumstance, or human nature in general?

10. Frieda has gone from acquiescence to her parents' traditions, her group leader's feminist ideals, and her husband's schemes, to acting on her own moral promptings. Will she continue to set her own course?

For complete discussion guides and author contact information,
visit www.rochlin-roots-west.com

DIANA LIVELY IS FALLING DOWN

Author: *Sheila Curran*

Publisher: Penguin, 2005

Website: www.sheilacurran.com

Available in:
Paperback, 427 pages. $14.00
ISBN 0-425-20242-9

Subject: Motherhood/Marriage/
Gender/Grief/Environment (Fiction)

Summary: Diana Lively—a talented British architect who builds doll-houses so she can tend to the needs of her three children and demanding husband—finds her world turned upside down when an American entrepreneur invites her family to live in Arizona for a year.

"Diana Lively Is Falling Down *is a real pick-me-up. One British woman crosses the pond to find herself a fish-out-of-water—only to realize that for the first time in her life, she can stand on her own two feet. Filled with characters who make you laugh out loud even as they break your heart, this is a funny, warm, inventive, original book.*" —**Jodi Picoult, author of** *Vanishing Acts* **and** *My Sister's Keeper*

"*Filled with exceptional characterization, Curran's novel gently reminds readers that fantasy has a place in everyone's life. . . . This is a gem.*" —*Booklist*, **starred review**

"*Brilliant, touching and funny as hell.*"—**Carlos Eire, 2003 National Book Award Winner for** *Waiting for Snow in Havana.*

Sheila Curran is a writer, mother and faculty wife who lives in Talla-hassee, Florida. Her experience as a trailing spouse in Oxford, England, and Phoenix, Arizona, provided the backdrop for this novel.

Topics for Discussion

1. In the first chapter, when Ted shows Wally the picture of the knight Gawain, whose compassionate impulse freed his wife from a spell, Wally says, almost to himself, "Kind of about faith, if you think about it." Later, when he and Diana picnic on the land overlooking the Dreamy Draw, they discuss their somewhat fragile understanding of the supernatural. What do they mean by faith, and what role does it play in explaining the behaviors of the characters? In the end, would you say Wally's faith was warranted or not?

2. How do you explain Audrey's attachment to the idea that her mother and she have Native American blood? Is it connected to her desire to return the world to a more innocent state, wherein mother nature is respected? Do other characters romanticize the past, and if so, are they fools or heroes for doing so?

3. Humphrey's mannerisms and interests are very feminine, from his devotion to Martha Stewart to the nurturing that he showers on Diana and Audrey. Is his sexuality, as it plays out at the end, believable? If so, do you think such a character would be possible in another era, before the push for gender equality in contemporary life? If your child were like Humphrey, would you encourage his nurturing traits, or fear for his emotional survival?

4. What does motherhood mean for the various characters in the novel? For example, how does Wally's reverence for his own mother translate to his relationship with Mary Kate and her alcoholism? For Diana, how does her sense of what children need from parents play into her relationship with Ted? Is Mary Kate's dramatic choice an act of love or selfishness? Is it forgivable?

5. What role does guilt play in motivating the characters' actions? How does it operate as both a negative and positive force for them?

6. What is the author's attitude towards fantasy? Is it simply escapist in nature, providing a means of escape from the more difficult parts of life, or does it inspire the characters to do things they previously felt were impossible? For example, how does William's fantasy that Johnny is his father help to keep alive Wally's suspicion that his wife has reached out from death to give him a message? How does Wally's fantasy of the perfect theme park both blind him to certain facts and simultaneously allow him to triumph over Ted's sabotage?

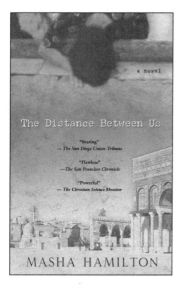

THE DISTANCE BETWEEN US

Author: *Masha Hamilton*

Publisher: Unbridled Books, 2005

Website: www.unbridledbooks.com

Available in:
Paperback, 304 pages. $14.95
ISBN 1-932961-14-3
Hardcover, 304 pages. $24.95 (2004)
ISBN 1-932961-02-X

Subject: Middle East/Journalism/
Love Story (Fiction)

Summary: After Middle Eastern war correspondent Caddie Blair loses her colleague and lover in an ambush, she is devastated by grief and unmoored by the sudden loss of her journalistic detachment. Operating without her normal instinct and internal compass, Caddie becomes a member of the community, no longer an outsider, and therefore increasingly vulnerable and volatile, especially in the face of her growing desire for revenge. Illuminating and perceptive, *The Distance Between Us* is as relevant and timely as it is powerful and gripping.

A *Library Journal* Book of the Year, 2004

"[A] great story . . . Will get you thinking and break your heart."
—**iVillage.com**

"Searing."—*The San Diego Union-Tribune*

Masha Hamilton worked as a foreign correspondent for ten years in the Middle East and Moscow. She wrote a newspaper column from Moscow and reported for NBC/Mutual Radio. Masha covered the intefadeh, the peace process, and the partial Israeli withdrawal from Lebanon. Later, she reported on the coup and collapse of the Soviet Union and the growing independence in Soviet republics as well as Kremlin politics. She reported from Afghanistan in the spring 2004 and now works as an editor on the Associated Press foreign desk. Her first novel, *Staircase of a Thousand Steps,* was a Book Sense 76 Pick and a Barnes & Noble Discover Great New Writers selection.

Topics for Discussion

1. What are some of the historical and cultural differences that create distance between the Palestinians and the Jews in this story? How does creating distance influence Caddie's relationship with Marcus? her professional colleagues? her friends? her community? herself?

2. In an instant, Caddie loses the two elements of her life most dear to her: Marcus and her professional detachment. How has reporting about violence in the past affected her?

3. After Marcus's death, Caddie finds herself drawn closer and closer to dangerous situations. What drives this reckless behavior? What other professions encourage similar forms of escape?

4. What is behind Caddie's strong attraction to Goronsky?

5. Lingering thoughts of revenge plague Caddie. Did you expect this?

6. The female characters in this novel—including Ya'el, Sarah, Halima, Anya—are diverse women who represent many cultures and values. How does each affect Caddie's actions and influence her decisions?

7. Memories of Marcus's death haunt Caddie. Is she in any way responsible for his death, or is she struggling with her own guilt for surviving the ambush? How does Marcus's journal—and perhaps his death—help her to heal?

8. Sarah tells Caddie, "Two kinds of people find their way to this place. Those who leave, and those who stay." Does Caddie's decision surprise you? How do her personal and professional losses reshape her life?

9. This fictional account of violence in the Middle East parallels many real-life, contemporary scenarios, both at home and abroad (for example, the war in Iraq, September 11, Columbine High School, Kosovo, Sarajevo, and Sudan). What motivates the kind of coverage given to these events? Is the reporting informative or voyeuristic?

10. This book is dedicated to Kevin Carter, a photojournalist who won a Pulitzer Prize for his disturbing photo of the famine in Sudan. In the picture, a gaunt Sudanese child crouches low to the ground while a vulture lurks nearby. Not long after winning the Pulitzer, Carter took his life. As a strict observer, journalists sometimes may have to let violence and brutality occur because if they become involved, they may change the outcome of the event or the public's understanding of a situation. Are there situations when a journalist should become a participant or is it better to remain an observer?

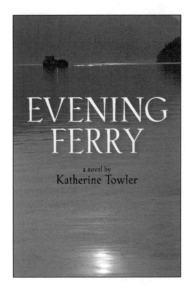

EVENING FERRY

Author: *Katherine Towler*

Publisher: MacAdam/Cage Publishing, 2005

Website: www.macadamcage.com

Available in:
Hardcover, 378 pages. $25.00
ISBN 1-59692-124-2

Subject: Americana/Love/Women/ Family Relationships/Small-town Life (Fiction)

Summary: Following the success of *Snow Island* (2002), Katherine Towler returns to the fictional New England island with *Evening Ferry*— the second installment of the multi-generational trilogy about family bonds, unexpected love, and the threat of war.

In the summer of 1965, Rachel returns to Snow Island to care for her injured father and discovers her mother's diaries hidden in a closet. Reading Phoebe Shattuck's account of her life as a wife and a mother, Rachel learns the truth about her own family's history, her mother's death, and her own aspirations to lead a new life.

In elegant prose and inspired storytelling, Towler gives us a moving portrait of two women and the island they come to call home, at a time when the world is changing and a new generation faces war.

"Inner quandaries over love, sex, memories, dreams and codes of duty are rendered with a light but vivid elegance . . . by intertwining each era's history and cultural shifts with the stories of individual islanders, Towler is creating a memorable regional trilogy."—**Providence Journal**

Katherine Towler is the author of the novel *Snow Island*. She completed her undergraduate degree at the University of Michigan and graduate degrees at Johns Hopkins and Middlebury College. A freelance writer, she lives in New Hampshire.

Topics for Discussion

1. Rachel Shattuck is at a crossroads at the opening of *Evening Ferry*, after her recent divorce and the death of her mother. How would you describe where she stands at the book's end and the journey she has made?

2. The structure of the novel presents two voices—Rachel's point of view and the first person voice of Phoebe in the diaries—and two time periods. How do the shifts in voice and time affect your understanding of both Rachel and Phoebe? Is the structure of the book effective and what does it achieve?

3. Why does Nate want Rachel to read her mother's diaries? And why does Rachel read them in secret, trying to prevent her father from discovering that she has read them?

4. The Vietnam War hovers in the background of the story. Is the war significant? Why do you think the author set this book in 1965 and 1966 rather than 1969 or the early 1970s, when American involvement and anti-war sentiment were at their strongest?

5. Phoebe struggles with her role as a mother, especially to Andy, her disabled child. Is Phoebe's response to being a mother surprising? Did her handling of the decision to institutionalize Andy change your understanding of Phoebe in any way?

6. Readers have commented that the island itself is a character in both *Snow Island* and *Evening Ferry*. Do you think this is true? How does the island setting inform the story? Could this story take place somewhere else?

7. At the end of the book, do you think that Rachel's relationship with her father has changed? What has Rachel learned and how do you think it will affect her understanding of herself and her father in the future? How does it affect her understanding of her mother as well?

8. *Evening Ferry* is the second volume of a proposed trilogy. Why do you think Katherine Towler chose to jump 20 years ahead of *Snow Island* in this volume and to focus on a different set of main characters? What does this achieve?

9. War is an underlying theme in *Snow Island* and *Evening Ferry*. How does Katherine Towler explore this theme?

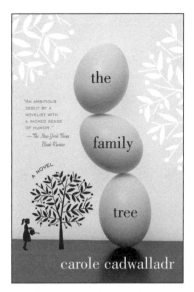

THE FAMILY TREE

Author: *Carole Cadwalladr*

Publisher: Plume Books
December 2005

Website: www.penguin.com
www.Cadwalladr.com

Available in:
Paperback, 400 pages. $14.00
ISBN 0-452-28694-8

Subject: Women's Lives/Identity/
Relationships (Fiction)

Summary: When Rebecca Monroe—married to Alistair, a scientist who doesn't believe in fate, but rather genetic disposition—discovers that she is pregnant, she begins to question what makes us who we are and whether her own precarious family history will play a role in her future.

For Rebecca, the wry and observant narrator of *The Family Tree*, simple things said over breakfast take on greater meaning; a home-improvement project foreshadows darker things to come; the color of one's eyes, the slope of a forehead are all missing pieces to the truth behind the family tree.

At once nostalgic and refreshingly original, *The Family Tree* is a sophisticated story of one woman and the generations of women who came before her and whose legacy shaped her life and its emotional landscape.

"Poignant and amusing. . . . While some have labeled The Family Tree *chick lit, don't be fooled: In fact, this is lit that happens to be written by one very clever chick."—**People***

Carole Cadwalladr writes for newspapers including *The Daily Telegraph* and has been nominated for the Best Specialist Writer/British Press Awards. *The Family Tree* is her first novel.

Topics for Discussion

1. At the start of *The Family Tree* we are introduced to Rebecca's early fascination with words and their definitions. This fascination is fundamental to the book's structure—sections and chapters often begin with definitions of words that relate to the particular section of chapter's content. Discuss the structure of the book and the role of the words Rebecca defines. How do they influence your interpretation of the text? Because she does not often give the entire definition of a word, what is significant about the parts of the definition she does reveal?

2. At the end of the novel, Rebecca reveals the truth about her mother's relationship with Kenneth and her father's relationship with Suzanne. She says, "You can retrofit all you like, but the clues weren't there, I've checked. That's the problem with point-of-view narrative." In light of her theory about point-of-view narrative, discuss the "clues" scattered throughout the book about her relationship with Alistair. How early in the story can we see the relationship's demise? Did her explanation about opposites attracting ever seem valid? How much do we "see" as readers that Rebecca does not as the novel progresses?

3. Motherhood, and the complicated relationship that exists between mother and daughter, is as central to the book as the arguments about genetic inheritance and learned behavior. Compare the relationships between all the respective mothers and daughters. Where do these relationships mirror one another, and where do they diverge? What hopes do we have for Rebecca at the book's culmination, as she becomes a mother to a daughter herself?

4. Is Herbert a sympathetic character? Discuss his obsessive-compulsive behavior and his preoccupation with his cousin. In light of Doreen's diagnosis, what can we or do we infer about genetic inheritance?

5. Consider Rebecca's desire for and decision to have a baby in the face of Alistair's genetic evidence and opposition. Was Rebecca wise to have a child knowing the odds her offspring would inherit certain undesirable traits? What would you do in her place?

6. Consider how each character of the book supports the argument for either Nature or Nurture. Which side of the argument has "won"—Nature or Nurture? Of which do you think Cadwalladr is a proponent? Why? What is her final "message" of the book?

For complete reading group guide, visit www.penguin.com.

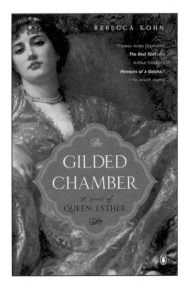

THE GILDED CHAMBER
A novel of Queen Esther

Author: *Rebecca Kohn*

Publisher: Penguin, 2005

Website: www.rebeccakohn.com

Available in:
Paperback, 368 pages. $14.00
ISBN 0-14-303533-9

Subject: Jewish Interest/Women's Lives (Fiction)

Summary: For centuries her name has been a byword for feminine beauty, guile, and wisdom. This sweeping, meticulously researched novel restores Esther to her full, complex humanity while reanimating the glittering Persian Empire in which her story unfolded. Esther comes to that land as a terrified Jewish orphan betrothed to her cousin, a well-connected courtier. She finds a world racked by intrigue and unfathomable hatreds and realizes that the only way to survive is to win the heart of its king. Passionate, suspenseful, and historically authentic, *The Gilded Chamber* illuminates the dilemma of a woman torn between her heart and her sense of duty, resulting in pure narrative enchantment.

"The Gilded Chamber *is a world unto itself and one well worth entering.*"
—**Margaret George, author of** *Mary, Called Magdalene*

"Rebecca Kohn takes us into places that the Old Testament never dreamed of. . . . A triumph of historical imagination and a must-read for lovers—and lovers of Jewish history." —**Steven Pressfield, author of** *Gates of Fire*

"Fans of Orson Scott Card's Sarah *and Anita Diamant's* The Red Tent *have a new author to follow in Kohn."* —**Library Journal**

"Evocatively and sensuously told." —**Booklist**

Rebecca Kohn lives in Hanover, New Hampshire, with her husband and daughter. This is her first novel.

Topics for Discussion

1. Were you surprised to learn there was such an important queen in such an ancient court and such a strong heroine in the Bible?

2. As queen, Esther is part of a decadent world of material things. What enables Esther to remember that riches are not the most important part of life?

3. At times it is easy to forget that Esther, the pampered queen, is also a slave forbidden to leave the palace confines. How would it feel to always be indoors and never allowed out?

4. Esther is torn between her desire to stop the decree against the Jewish people and her need to maintain her own safety and that of those that she cares about and already has responsibility for, such as Vadhut and Puah. Though she has limited options, Esther in her own way has power. Discuss some points in the novel when she exercises that power. What would you do in her position?

5. One of the most interesting issues in the book is the need for various characters to hide their Jewish origins. What is at stake for them in muting their backgrounds? What strategies do they employ for maintaining their faith and their heritage? What factors drive some of the characters to finally reveal their religion?

6. This is quite a realistic love story, in which emotional relations are complicated by issues of gender and power. What does Esther gain from Mordechai and the king, and what does each deny her? Who do you think she is more suited for?

7. Why doesn't Mordechai marry Esther when she comes of age? Does he change over the course of the novel? Do you think that he does love and wish to marry Esther? Does the end of the story bring him redemption?

8. What does Ester need to gain in order to be fulfilled by the end of the novel?

9. The novel ends with Esther embarking on a new phase in her life. Can you imagine what her life might be like? What aspects of daily life do you think she values most?

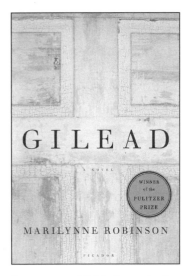

GILEAD

Author: *Marilynne Robinson*

Publisher: Picador USA, January 2006

Website: www.picadorusa.com

Available in:
Paperback, 256 pages, $14.00
ISBN 0-312-42440-X

Subject: American Culture/
Small-town Life/Christianity (Fiction)

Summary: Told through the eyes of a Midwestern minister nearing the end of his life, *Gilead* unfolds in the form of a letter. As Reverend Ames writes to his young son, we learn of the family's legacy, a heritage steeped in abolition, economic hardship, and conflicting views on religion and war as each generation comes of age. The 1950s find John Ames comparing his grandfather, a fiery Union Army chaplain, to his devoutly pacifist father while a gentle turn of events poses the question of racial equality in new terms. Throughout the novel, he recalls a life shaped by love—for his faith, his vocation and his church, for prayer, for his town and all it has meant, for his father and grandfather, for his books, for baseball, for his lifelong friends, for his physical life and the splendors of the physical world, for his memories, and for the young wife and infant child to whom he remains loyal over solitary decades.

"Gilead is a beautiful work—demanding, grave and lucid. . . . Gradually, Robinson's novel teaches us how to read it, suggests how we might slow down to walk at its own processional pace, and how we might learn to coddle its many fine details." —**James Wood**, *The New York Times Book Review*

Marilynne Robinson is the author of *Housekeeping*, winner of the PEN/Hemingway Award for First Fiction, and released as a major motion picture in 1987. She has also written two nonfiction books: *Mother Country*, an examination of Great Britain's role in environmental pollution, and *The Death of Adam*, a collection of essays on religion, history, and the state of society. She has an undergraduate degree from Brown University and a Ph.D. in English literature from the University of Washington. She teaches at the University of Iowa Writers' Workshop.

Topics for Discussion

1. What was your perception of the narrator in the opening paragraphs? In what ways did your understanding of him change throughout the novel? Did John's own perception of his life seem to evolve as well?

2. Biblical references to Gilead (a region near the Jordan River) describe its plants as having healing properties. The African-American spiritual, "There Is a Balm in Gilead," equates Jesus with this balm. According to some sources, the Hebrew origin of the word simply means "rocky area." Do these facts make *Gilead* an ironic or symbolically accurate title for the novel?

3. The vision experienced by John's grandfather is a reminder that the Christ he loves identifies utterly with the oppressed and afflicted whom he must therefore help to free. What guides John in discerning his own mission?

4. How does John feel about his brother's atheism in retrospect? What accounts for Edward's departure from the church? What enabled John to retain his faith?

5. The rituals of communion and baptism provide many significant images throughout the novel. What varied meanings do John and his parishioners ascribe to them?

6. What answers would you have given to the questions John faces regarding the fate of souls and the nature of pain in the world?

7. Marilynne Robinson included several quotations from Scripture and hymns; John expresses particular admiration for Isaac Watts, an eighteenth-century English minister whose hymns were widely adopted by various Protestant denominations. Are certain texts divinely inspired? What is the role of metaphor in communicating about spiritual matters?

8. Discuss the literary devices used in this novel, such as its epistolary format, John's finely honed voice, and the absence of conventional chapter breaks (save for a long pause before Jack's marriage is revealed). How would you characterize *Gilead*'s narrative structure?

9. Is there a difference between the ways religion manifests itself in small towns versus urban locales? Did the history of Iowa's rural communities and the strain of radicalism in Midwestern history surprise you?

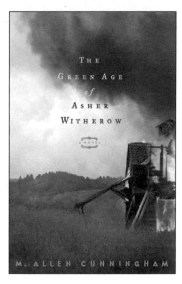

THE GREEN AGE OF ASHER WITHEROW

Author: *M. Allen Cunningham*

Publisher: Unbridled Books, 2005

Website: www.unbridledbooks.com

Available in:
Paperback, 288 pages. $14.95
ISBN 1-932961-13-5
Hardcover, 288 pages. $24.95 (2004)
ISBN 1-932961-00-3

Subject: California/Coal Mining/
Coming of Age (Fiction)

Summary: In this mesmerizing first novel by a gifted young writer, the drama of California's rich immigrant history and the freshness and wonder of childhood combine with darker elements of legend, magic and mystery. Born while the Civil War is raging further east, young Asher Witherow seems marked for an extraordinary future. Anything but typical, he captures the attention of the eerily watchful apprentice minister and schoolteacher, Josiah Lyte, and of young Thomas Motion, a strange boy who can see into the deepest darkness. When Thomas mysteriously vanishes, only Asher knows the truth of what has happened to him, and he must decide whether to keep his knowledge secret or reveal what he believes to be his own unforgivable mistake. It is an agonizing moral decision that will forever affect the lives of those closest to him and that will ultimately have a profound impact on all of Nortonville.

#1 *Book Sense* **Pick for October 2004**

"Compelling and . . . artfully told."—The St. Louis Post-Dispatch

"Vivid in character . . . impressive."—The San Jose Mercury News

M. Allen Cunningham published this novel at age 26. His work has appeared in a number of literary magazines, including *Glimmer Train, Boulevard, Epoch,* and *Alaska Quarterly Review*. His short fiction has been nominated for two Pushcart Prizes. Cunningham, who has not studied writing formally, lived for nearly two decades in the Diablo Valley region of California, where this novel is set. He now lives in Portland, Oregon.

Topics for Discussion

1. Why is the natural landscape of the Diablo Valley so important, especially to the younger characters in the novel?

2. Several myths, legends and systems of belief are mentioned in the novel. There is the traditional Protestant Christianity of Reverend Parry and the Nortonville residents; there is Josiah Lyte's own unique version of Christianity; there is the Hinduism that influences him during his childhood in India; there are the Native American legends of Indian tribes that first named the mountain and the Celtic myths and stories of Asher's Welsh ancestors. How do these "underpinnings" inform the story?

3. Sarah Norton is a disturbing character in the novel. As a midwife (and, in Anna's case, an abortionist), she is suspected by some people in Nortonville of being a witch. Why do you think the author "drew" her this way?

4. The coal miners of Nortonville are a proud people. What seems to be the nature of that pride, and what are its main sources?

5. Asher's mother, Abicca, is among the many citizens of Nortonville who believe the young minister, Josiah Lyte, is ungodly and dangerous, not just *different*. Does Josiah Lyte pose a real threat to the town?

6. Why is Josiah Lyte so interested in Asher? Is it simply because the boy is a gifted student, or is there more to it than that? Why does Lyte refuse to tell anyone how Thomas disappeared and what role Asher played?

7. Thomas Motion teaches Asher to see in the dark. This ability abandons both Asher and Thomas once they are underground. Why can't they see in the dark there? Why do you think Anna Flood has this gift?

8. What draws Asher to Anna Flood? Why is Anna so certain that they will be friends? How do the events cause their relationship to develop?

9. This is a historical novel, with many realistic details of nineteenth-century California and the mining town of Nortonville. Yet certain elements of the story are more magical than real. Why do you think the author chose to include these elements of magic and mystery?

10. The elder Asher gives us hints about his life between the time Nortonville's mining industry declined and he left the town until the present time (1950) when he is writing his story. What do you imagine may have happened to him in the years in between? What do you think has driven him to write the story of his early years in Nortonville?

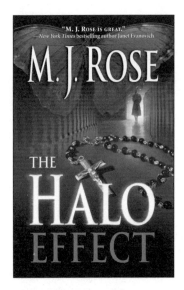

THE HALO EFFECT

Author: *M.J. Rose*

Publisher: Mira Books, 2005

Website: www.mjrose.com

Available in:
Mass Market, 384 pages, $6.99
ISBN 0-77832-197-5
Paperback, 352 pages. $12.95
ISBN 0-77832-080-4

Subject: Mystery/Suspense/Thriller/
Sex Therapy (Fiction)

Summary: Nominated for the an Anthony Award for Best Original Paper-pack and an international bestseller, *The Halo Effect* features sex therapist, Dr. Morgan Snow. She struggles with the conflict of preserving her patient's privacy and the dangerous and sometimes criminal things she hears. When a killer starts murdering prostitutes, the first one being a patient of Morgan, and then Cleo Thane, a high-class call girl and patient, disappears; Morgan feels compelled to take action.

Dr. Snow sees everything from the abused to the depraved, from the couples grappling with sexual boredom to twisted sociopaths with dark, erotic fetishes and the Butterfield Institute is the sanctuary where she helps soothe and heal these battered souls.

"*The Halo Effect will keep you spellbound and guessing from the first page to the last.*" —*Kirkus Reviews*

"*Dr. Morgan Snow is a refreshingly vulnerable character whose spunky decision to go undercover in the demimonde is both believable and hair-raising.* The Halo Effect *will have you on the edge of your seat from page one.*" —**Katherine Neville,** *New York Times* **bestselling author of** *The Eight*

M.J. Rose is the author of five novels, *Lip Service, In Fidelity, Flesh Tones, Sheet Music* and *The Halo Effect.* She also is a contributor to *Poets and Writers, Oprah Magazine, The Writer Magazine,* and *Pages Magazine.* Rose is also the co-author with Angela Adair Hoy of *How to Publish and Promote Online,* and with Doug Clegg of *Buzz Your Book.*

Topics for Discussion

1. Dr. Morgan Snow has been working as a psychiatrist for The Butterfield Institute for the last five years. One of her patients is a call girl named Cleo, who has succeeded in developing a business by herself and leads a comfortable life. Are there issues in both a therapist's life and a high class call girl's life that mirror each other?

2. How does the author switch back and forth between her narrative and the one done by Morgan make the novel more interesting? How do they make it easier to understand the motivations and logic behind the actions of Morgan?

3. When Special Victims Unit detective Noah Jordain contacts Morgan seeking her help in profiling the killer of the prostitutes, Morgan is placed between a rock and a hard place. If she talks, she breaches the confidence Cleo placed in her, but if she does not and Cleo is really in trouble, she is preventing her from getting help. How does this theme of doing the wrong thing for the right reason play out in this book? Do you think that Morgan made the right decision?

4. What makes this novel more of a whydunit than a whodunit? Do we do titles a disservice by classifying them? Or is classifying them in genres like mystery, romance, literary, important for readers? What does transcending a genre mean?

5. *The Halo Effect* is a psychological/erotic thriller with many references to sex and religion and the roles they play in today's society. What do you think of the hot buttons Rose has brought to light in the book?

6. How did the relationship between Morgan and her daughter, and her relationship with Nina, and her relationship with Detective Jordain enhance your understanding of what drove Morgan to take the chances she did in the book?

7. Is sex a difficult subject to write about without getting gritty and too realistic? Did the sexuality in the book disturb you or give you a greater understanding of the characters and add to the story?

8. Why do you think the author called the novel *The Halo Effect*?

9. So, would you go to Dr. Morgan Snow if you had a problem? Why or why not?

THE HISTORY OF LOVE

Author: *Nicole Krauss*

Publisher: W.W. Norton, April 2006

Website: www.wwnorton.com

Available in:
Paperback, 320 pages. $13.95
ISBN 0-393-32862-7
Hardcover, 320 pages. $23.95 (2005)
ISBN 0-393-06034-9

Subject: Books and Reading/
Immigrants/Lost Literature (Fiction)

Summary: Leo Gursky is just about surviving, tapping his radiator each evening to let his upstairs neighbor know he's still alive. But life wasn't always like this: sixty years ago, in the Polish village where he was born, Leo fell in love and wrote a book. And though Leo doesn't know it, that book survived, inspiring fabulous circumstances, even love. Fourteen-year-old Alma was named after a character in that very book. She undertakes an adventure to find her namesake and save her family. With consummate, spellbinding skill, Nicole Krauss gradually draws together their stories.

Inspired by the author's four grandparents and by a pantheon of authors, such as Bruno Schulz, Franz Kafka, and Isaac Babel, this book is truly a history of love—a tale brimming with laughter, irony, passion, and soaring imaginative power.

"Beyond the vigorous whiplash that keeps Ms. Krauss's History of Love *moving (and keeps its reader off balance until a stunning finale), this novel is tightly packed with ingenious asides. . . . Even at their most odd-ball, these flourishes reflect the deep, surprising wisdom that gives this novel its ultimate heft. . . . Ms. Krauss's work is illuminated by the warmth and delicacy of her prose."* —**Janet Maslin,** *New York Times*

Nicole Krauss was born in New York in 1974. Her first novel *Man Walks into a Room* was named Book of the Year by the *Los Angeles Times*. Her fiction has appeared in the *New Yorker, Esquire,* and *Best American Short Stories*. She lives in Brooklyn.

Topics for Discussion

1. Leo fears becoming invisible. How does fiction writing prove a balm for his anxiety?

2. Despite his preoccupation with his approaching death, Leo has a spirit that is indefatigably comic. Describe the interplay of tragedy and comedy in *The History of Love*.

3. What distinguishes parental love from romantic love in the novel?

4. Uncle Julian tells Alma, "Wittgenstein once wrote that when the eye sees something beautiful, the hand wants to draw it." How does this philosophical take on the artistic process relate to the impulse to write in *The History of Love*?

5. Many different narrators contribute to the story of *The History of Love*. What makes each of their voices unique? How does Krauss seam them together to make a coherent novel?

6. Survival requires different tactics in different environments. Aside from Alma's wilderness guidelines, what measures do the characters in the novel adopt to carry on?

7. Most all of the characters in the novel are writers—from Isaac Moritz to Bird Singer. Alma's mother is somewhat exceptional, as she works as a translator. Yet she is not the only character to transform others' words for her creative practice. What are the similarities and differences between an author and a translator?

8. The fame and adulation Isaac Moritz earns for his novels represent the rewards many writers hope for, while Leo, an unwitting ghostwriter, remains unrecognized for his work. What role does validation play in the many acts of writing in *The History of Love*?

9. Leo decides to model nude for an art class in order to leave an imprint of his existence. He writes to preserve the memories of his love for Alma Mereminski. Yet drawings and novels are never faithful renditions of the truth. Do you recognize a process of erasure in the stories he tells us?

10. Why might Krauss have given her novel the title *The History of Love*, the same as that of the fictional book around which her narrative centers?

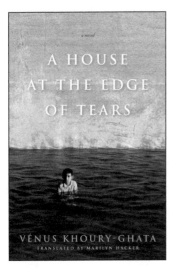

A HOUSE AT THE EDGE OF TEARS

Translated from the French by Marilyn Hacker

Author: *Vénus Khoury-Ghata*

Publisher: Graywolf Press, November 2005

Website: www.graywolfpress.org

Available in:
Paperback, 128 pages. $12.00
ISBN 1-55597-434-1

Subject: French Studies/Arabic Studies/Middle Eastern Studies (Fiction)

Summary: In the city of Beirut, five shabby dwellings circle a courtyard with a pomegranate tree weeping blood red fruit. The residents hear screams in the night as a boy is beaten by his father—a punishment for masturbating in his sleep. A crime not worthy of the punishment: the neighbors gossip and decide that he must have tried to rape his sisters. The poems he writes are perhaps an even greater crime to his father, but ultimately a gift to his eldest sister, who narrates their story with a combination of brutal truth and stunning prose.

In this mesmerizing novel, celebrated novelist and poet, Khoury-Ghata, presents the disintegration of a family and a country—both ruled by a fury fueled by fear.

"I found A House at the Edge of Tears *stunning and provocative, compelling and haunting. Vénus Khoury-Ghata has weaved like a lace maker the story of her brother, herself, her family, and a society far removed from any bland ideal . . . using the finest, poetic, hypnotic prose which pricks you like needles."*—**Hanan al-Shaykh**

Vénus Khoury-Ghata was crowned Miss Lebanon in 1959. She was married twice—once to a very wealthy Lebanese man and later to a scientist in Paris. Khoury-Ghata spent many of her childhood summers in Lebanon, where she lived in the house next door to the prophet Khalil Gibran. Vénus Khoury-Ghata's *She Says*, which was also translated by Marilyn Hacker, was recently published in the United States and named a Finalist for the National Book Critics Circle Award for Poetry. Vénus Khoury-Ghata rarely goes back to Beirut and writes only in French.

Topics for Discussion

1. What kind of city is Khoury-Ghata's Beirut? How does multicultural-ism shape its social structure and citizens' identities? How do the locals view foreigners? What is the role of Westernization, and does it affect the city dwellers' values, actions, and lives?

2. The main character is interested in beauty and the arts; beauty queens, the tango, poetry. How important are appearances? Is beauty in integral part of the village life? Why does the main character enter beauty contests?

3. Discuss the book's maternal figures. Are there similarities between the narrator's mother and the weeping Madonna? Does inaction in the face of a tyrannical husband make this mother a martyr or, as the brother suggests, a tacit conspirator? How responsible are parents for their children's fates?

4. The narrator tells her brother that she wrote "with your pen, on the page that you hadn't been able to fill." How much of this book was written for her brother? For whom else does she speak? Why would the narrator choose to write such a book?

5. From the pulpy red pomegranate tree to the stained sheets at Renee's childbirth, Khoury-Ghata frequently uses the imagery of blood. Are the bloody scenes related? How do blood's traditional connotations—violence, passion, and family lineage, for instance—interact with Khoury-Ghata's discussion of it? How does the brother's "blood disease," or heroin addiction, connect to this theme?

6. Is the father's "curse of the monastery" fulfilled? Does religion "curse" or empower characters that believe? Could the Vinikoffs' hunt for treasure be read as a leap of faith, since they cannot be certain that the treasure truly exists? Are we to admire or pity the Vinikoffs' efforts?

7. The main characters in this book are required to speak formal French instcad of street French or Arabic. Do literacy and multilingualism alienate them from their community? Does it help them? The narrator's brother's relationship with language changes over the course of time: What is the relevance of his linguistic degeneration? How do the boy's rebellion and illness affect the family's views on literature and education?

8. The narrator frequently moves from Beirut to a small village in the countryside. How does this change the narrator?

Photo by Kieran Harnett

IF YOU COULD SEE ME NOW

Author: *Cecelia Ahern*

Publisher: Hyperion Books
January 2006

Website: www.cecelia-ahern.com

Available in:
Hardcover, 384 pages. $22.95
ISBN 1-4013-0187-8

Subject: Ireland (Fiction)

Summary: In her third novel, bestselling author Cecelia Ahern introduces us to two sisters at odds with each other. Elizabeth's life is an organized mess. The organized part is all due to her own efforts. The mess is entirely due to her sister, Saoirse, whose personal problems leave Elizabeth scrambling to pick up the pieces. One of these pieces is Saoirse's six-year-old son, Luke. Luke is quiet and contemplative, until the arrival of a new friend, Ivan, turns him into an outgoing, lively kid. And Elizabeth's life is about to change in wonderful ways she has only dreamed of.

With all the warmth and wit that fans have come to expect from Cecelia Ahern, this is a novel full of magic, heart, and surprising romance.

Praise for Cecelia Ahern's previous novel *PS, I Love You*:
"Sweet and sad and funny: a charming journey of grief and hope."
—**Marian Keyes, author of *Sushi for Beginners***

Cecelia Ahern, the 23-year-old daughter of Ireland's prime minister, holds a degree in Journalism and Media Communications. The author of *PS, I Love You* and *Love, Rosie*, she lives in Dublin, Ireland.

Topics for Discussion

1. Who was Ivan sent to befriend—Elizabeth or Luke? Who's life does he change more?

2. Did you have an imaginary friend? How did he change your outlook on life?

3. At the end of the book, Elizabeth finally confronts her childhood. How does that change how she thinks about life? How did her childhood memory align with what really happens? How can memory cloud your reality?

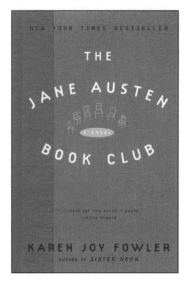

THE JANE AUSTEN BOOK CLUB

Author: *Karen Joy Fowler*

Publisher: Plume Books, 2005

Website: www.penguin.com

Available in:
Paperback, 304 pages. $14.00
ISBN 0-452-28653-0

Subject: Women's Lives/Friendship (Fiction)

Summary: In California's Central Valley, five women and one man meet to discuss Jane Austen's novels. Over the six months they get together, marriages are tested, affairs begin, unsuitable arrangements become suitable, and love happens. With her eye for the frailties of human behavior and her ear for the absurdities of social intercourse, Karen Joy Fowler has never been wittier or her characters more appealing. The result is a delicious dissection of modern relationships.

Dedicated Austenites will delight in unearthing the echoes of Austen that run through the novel, but most readers will simply enjoy the vision and voice that, despite two centuries of separation, unite two great writers of brilliant social comedy.

"Karen Joy Fowler creates a novel that is so winning, so touching, so delicately, slyly witty that admirers of Persuasion *and* Emma *will simply sigh with happiness."* —**Michael Dirda***, The Washington Post Book World*

Karen Joy Fowler, a PEN/Faulkner and Dublin IMPAC nominee, is the author of *The Sweetheart Season, Black Glass: Short Fictions*, as well as *Sarah Canary* and *Sister Noon* (available from Plume). She lives in Davis, California.

Topics for Discussion

1. The author opens the novel with a quote from Jane Austen, part of which reads, "Seldom, very seldom does complete truth belong to any human disclosure." Do you agree with this sentiment? Why do you think the author chooses to open the novel with this quote?

2. When the group is first being formed, Bernadette suggests that it should consist exclusively of women: "The dynamic changes with men. They pontificate rather than communicate. They talk more than their share." What do you think of her statement? How does Grigg affect the group's dynamic? How would things have been different without him?

3. While the group is reading *Sense and Sensibility* and discussing Mrs. Dashwood, Sylvia mentions that "the problems of older women don't interest most writers" and is thrilled that Austen seems to care. Do you agree with this, that most writers aren't interested in older women? What about society in general? How does Fowler approach older women? Later, Prudie says that "An older man can still fall in love. An older woman better not." Do you agree? How does Fowler deal with this issue?

4. Sylvia asks, "Why should unhappiness be so much more powerful than happiness?" How would you answer her?

5. The book club meets from March through August. How does the group change over these six months? "I always like to know how a story ends," Bernadette says. How do you think this story ends (the "epilogue to the epilogue")?

6. At the end of the novel, Jocelyn reluctantly agrees to read some science fiction, including the work of Ursula Le Guin, and really likes it. What other authors do you think the group might like? Although they would have to change the name of their group, what author would you suggest for the Central Valley/River City all-Jane-Austen-all-the-time book club to read next? What do you suggest for your own group?

7. If you're new to Jane Austen, are you now interested in reading her work? Based on what you've learned from Karen Jay Fowler, which novel would you go to first? If you are already a "dedicated Janeite," how has reading *The Jane Austen Book Club* made you feel about your favorite author? How would you describe your own "private Austen"? What novel would you recommend to first-time readers of Austen?

For complete reading group guide, visit www.penguin.com.

THE JUNGLE LAW

Author: *Victoria Vinton*

Publisher: MacAdam/Cage Publishing, 2005

Website: www.macadamcage.com

Available in:
Hardcover, 350 pages. $25.00
ISBN 1-59692-149-8

Subject: Books and Reading/Family Relationships/Rudyard Kipling (Fiction)

Summary: The author Rudyard Kipling is familiar to most, especially his famed stories that make up *The Jungle Book*. However, a lesser known fact is that although he was born in India, Rudyard Kipling came to live in Vermont in 1892 with his American wife and set up home in Brattleboro. It was there that he wrote *The Jungle Book*, inspired by his love for the country of his birth.

Victoria Vinton's *The Jungle Law* is a fictional account of the time the Kiplings spent in Vermont. Mixing fact and invention, Vinton parallels Kipling's story with that of his neighbors', the Connollys, who, like Kipling, came to Vermont to forge a better life but who are forced to question the decisions they have made in the wake of Kipling's presence in their lives.

*"Vinton mines a rich vein of intensity whether writing about landscape and weather, or the soul-expanding possibilities of creative life . . . radiantly colored, sensuous, respectful, and rapt; an impressive debut."—**Kirkus***

Victoria Vinton's short stories have appeared in publications such as *Sewanee Review* and *Prairie Schooner*. A recipient of an Artist Fellowship from the New York Foundation of the Arts and a Masters of Fine Arts degree in writing from Columbia, she lives with her daughter in Brooklyn, New York, where she works as a literacy consultant for the New York City Public Schools. *The Jungle Law* is her first book.

Topics for Discussion

1. Rudyard Kipling and Joe Connolly are both powerfully drawn to the idea of an orphaned boy raised by a family of wolves. What compels them so much about that idea? Are they drawn to it for the same or different reasons? And why do they also both seem to be drawn to the idea of a jungle ruled by strict laws?

2. What role does class play in the shaping of the characters' identities, their interactions with each other, and the unfolding of events?

3. Caroline Kipling is frequently portrayed in the novel as a controlling and imperious figure. Can she also be seen as a sympathetic character?

4. At the end of the book, Vinton gives us a portrait of the aged Rudyard Kipling without providing a similar picture of the other characters. What do you imagine might have happened to the Connollys during those intervening years and how does the omission of that information affect you as a reader? What might have been Vinton's reasons for not offering more about the Connollys?

5. Throughout much of the novel, Jack Connolly is motivated by anger and fear. What do you think he is really afraid of? What is he angry about?

6. In various ways the book explores the power of imagination, both as a vehicle for self-transformation and for self-deception? How do the different characters use that power for both positive and negative ends?

7. The last chapter takes place forty-three years after the events that precede it, with a picture of Rudyard Kipling as a dissatisfied and compromised man. Is that future foreseeable in the rest of the book, or—hindsight being hindsight, as Caroline Kipling says—can it only be seen retroactively?

8. Kipling ends his life still haunted by his years in the House of Desolation. Joe repeats certain journeys and actions of his father while believing himself a free agent. What do these and other incidents in the novel suggest about our ability to control our own fate? And how does the story of Mowgli support or counter those suggestions?

LIPSTICK JUNGLE

Author: *Candace Bushnell*

Publisher: Hyperion Books, 2005

Website: www.LipstickJungle.com
www.CandaceBushnell.com

Available in:
Hardcover, 416 pages, $24.95
ISBN 0-7868-6819-8

Subject: Female Relationships/
New York (Fiction)

Summary: Victory Ford is the darling of the fashion world. Single, attractive, and iconoclastic, she has worked for years to create her own signature line. As well as learning crucial lessons about what she really wants in a relationship.

Nico O'Neilly is the glamorous, brilliant editor of *Bonfire Magazine*— the pop-culture bible for fashion, show business, and politics. Considered one of the most powerful women in publishing, she seems to have it all. But in a mid-life crisis, she suddenly realizes this isn't enough.

Wendy Healy's chutzpah has propelled her to the very top of the cutthroat movie industry. When it becomes clear that a competitor is trying to oust her, something has to give—and Wendy must decide between her career and her marriage.

In *Lipstick Jungle*, Bushnell once again delivers an addictive pageturner of sex and scandal that will keep readers enthralled and guessing to the very last page.

"Bushnell's emphasis on female friendship and career ambition may . . . win her a legion of new readers. Her characters want 'the sweet, creamy sensation of power,' and it's Bushnell's account of how they got it, and how they keep it, that will really keep readers turning pages."
—Publishers Weekly

Candace Bushnell is the author of three bestsellers, *Sex and the City*, *Four Blondes*, and *Trading Up*. She has been a columnist for the *New York Observer* and a contributing editor to *Vogue*. She lives in New York City.

Topics for Discussion

1. Much of Bushnell's previous work is about a woman's quest to find and keep a man. But *Lipstick Jungle* focuses instead on the quest for power and success. What do you think of this decision? Does this book send a new type of message? What is it?

2. If you could have the life of Victory, Wendy, or Nico, which would you choose? Do you admire one of these characters more than the others? Why?

3. Would you ever consider Candace Bushnell a feminist? Why or why not?

4. What role does marriage play in the lives of these women? Does it help or hurt them? Or both?

5. What do you think about the men in this book? Are they characters or caricatures?

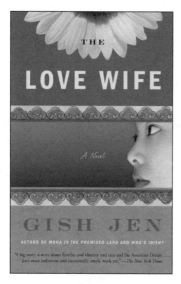

THE LOVE WIFE

Author: *Gish Jen*

Publisher: Vintage Books, 2005

Web site: www.readinggroupcenter.com

Available in:
Paperback, 400 pages. $14.00
ISBN 1-4000-7651-X

Subject: Family Life/Americana/
Culture & Identity (Fiction)

Summary: From the massively talented Gish Jen comes a barbed, moving, and stylistically dazzling new novel about the elusive nature of kinship. The Wongs describe themselves as a "half half" family, but the actual fractions are more complicated, given Carnegie's Chinese heritage, his wife Blondie's WASP background, and the various ethnic permutations of their adopted and biological children. Things get even more interesting with the arrival of Lanlan, Carnegie's Mainland Chinese relative who comes courtesy of Carnegie's mother's will. Is Lanlan a very good nanny, a heartless climber, or a posthumous gift from a formidable mother who never stopped wanting her son to marry a nice Chinese girl? Rich in insight, buoyed by humor, *The Love Wife* is a hugely satisfying work.

"A big story: a story about families and identity and race and the American Dream. . . . Jen's most ambitious and emotionally ample work yet."
—The New York Times

Gish Jen is the author of two previous novels and a book of stories. Her honors include the Lannan Award for Fiction and the Strauss Living Award from the American Academy of Arts and Letters. She lives with her husband and two children in Cambridge, Massachusetts.

Topics for Discussion

1. At the beginning of the novel, Blondie says, "At least I had my family. Every happy family has its innocence. I suppose, looking back, this was ours." Is her belief in the sanctity of the family shared by the others? In what ways does her upbringing and her position within the Bailey family influence her point of view?

2. Several decades separate the arrivals of Mama Wong and Lan in America. What insights do their backgrounds provide into the status of women in Chinese society both before and after the Communist takeover? How do their expectations and their experiences as immigrants differ?

3. What does Wendy's perspective add to our understanding of the family dynamics? What effect does the fact that she is adopted from China and her origins are clear have on the way she is treated by others and on her sense of self?

4. Does Lan's presence in the household alter Blondie and Carnegie's marriage in a fundamental way, or does it simply throw into relief differences that existed all along? Is the unraveling of the Wongs' marriage inevitable or does it confirm Blondie's suspicion that Mama Wong "would send us, from her grave, the wife [Carnegie] should have married"?

5. What personal ambitions did Lan bring to the United States? Is her drive and desire to make the most of herself admirable, or is it opportunistic and self-serving? How complicit is she in alienating Blondie from the family? What messages does she convey in the lessons she gives the girls in Chinese language and culture? What do her involvement with Shang and her marriage to Jeb Su reveal about Lan's priorities?

6. How do the juxtaposition of viewpoints and the mixture of tones affect the way the story unfolds and your reactions to the individual characters? Does a particular character stand out as the emotional center of the novel? How might a reader's own experience, gender, or background influence their sympathies for the various characters?

For a complete Reading Group Guide, visit www.readinggroupcenter.com

ADULT WOMEN WHO ARE STILL QUEEN BEES,
MIDDLE BEES, AND AFRAID-TO-BEES

mean girls grown up

Cheryl Dellasega, Ph.D., author of *Surviving Ophelia*

MEAN GIRLS GROWN UP
Adult Women Who Are Still Queen Bees, Middle Bees, and Afraid-to-Bees

Author: *Cheryl Dellasega*

Publisher: John Wiley & Sons, 2005

Website: www.wiley.com

Available in:
Hardcover, 256 pages. $24.95
ISBN 0-47165517-1

Subject: Self-Help/Psychology (Nonfiction)

Summary: Most women have experienced female aggression in one way or another, either as victim, aggressor, or bystander. In *Mean Girls Grown Up*, Cheryl Dellasega explores why women are often their own worst enemies, offering practical advice for dealing with aggressive behaviors in a variety of situations and for building healthy, positive relationships with other women.

Drawing upon extensive research and interviews, Dellasega shares stories from women around the world who have experienced relational aggression as well as the knowledge of experts have helped women overcome the bullying dynamic. From the PTA clique to the neighborhood carpool, from the gym to the boardroom, every woman know someone who is suffering from the devastating dynamic of relational aggression.

"Dr. Dellasega enlightens us about the sources of women's aggression towards each other and she provides us with extremely valuable tools for how to overcome our various roles in the hierarchy and learn more constructive and compassionate means to relate to other women."—**Debra Mandel, Ph.D., psychologist and author of *Healing the Sensitive Heart***

Cheryl Dellasega, Ph.D., is a professor in the College of Medicine and Department of Humanities at Pennsylvania State University. She lectures frequently on the subject of relational aggression and is the author of three previous books.

Topics for Discussion

1. Discuss relational aggression (RA). Is RA learned or "hard-wired?" Do women differ from men in the ways they express aggression? What motivations typically drive a woman to exhibit RA behavior? Is it possible to completely eliminate RA from your relationships?

2. What issues discussed in the book (i.e. the "PTA Clique," "Bully Boss," etc.) were especially relevant in your life?

3. What are the characteristics of Queen Bees you have known? Why might it be hard for a woman to admit to bullying Queen Bee behaviors? Ask yourself if you have been a Queen Bee (or are you still?). If so, how did (does) it make you feel to admit to this?

4. Who is more malicious—an overt Queen Bee or a behind-the-scenes Middle Bee? Who has more power? What advice might you have for women who find themselves in a bystander position but want to tactfully disengage from the Middle Bee role?

5. Have you ever been the target of false gossip? If so, describe how it impacted you. How did you respond?

6. The Afraid-to-Bee is the victim of other women's aggression. If you know an Afraid-to-Bee, what kind of advice can you give her so that her life is not completely derailed by a Queen Bee?

7. Are women tougher on female coworkers than male? If yes, why? Does an all-female working environment usually encourage or discourage the aggressor-victim dynamic? What other situations can you think of that spark competition among women? What can you do when your boss is Queen Bee?

8. The author offers numerous pointers in healing residual RA, such as confronting your aggressor, talking to a therapist, deciding to forgive, choosing compassion for your aggressor, and many more. What healing tools would work best for you and why? Does facing the past or present aggression really help someone to move on and create new, healthier relationships?

9. Think about some of today's most popular TV shows and movies. Do the media play a role in encouraging or discouraging RA between women? What do popular shows like *The Bachelor* and the plethora of reality shows—which draw viewers in with dramatic catfights and backstabbing—tell us about the way women are depicted in our culture?

ONE LAST DANCE
It's Never Too Late to Fall in Love

Author: *Mardo Williams*
(with his daughters, Kay & Jerri)

Publisher: Calliope Press, 2005

Website: www.CalliopePress.com

Available in:
Hardcover, 432 pages. $22.95
ISBN 0-9649241-4-5

Subject: Aging/Recovery/Love/
Sexuality/At-Risk Youth (Fiction)

Summary: Despite their disastrous first meeting, complete with a ruined birthday cake and insulting remarks, it was obvious to bystanders, even then, that Morgan, aged 89, and Dixie, 79, were fated for each other. The two begin to date and ultimately move in together—for economic reasons, they agree. But the business-only relationship changes and strengthens as the couple unite to combat illness, scandal, and a near-fatal accident.

The story is about finding love at any age, but also reveals how past insecurities, humiliations, and fears can haunt a person throughout his days. Dixie fears intimacy. Morgan has concealed important details about his divorce, his estranged children, and his lost job. And all the while, a mysterious intruder lurks, bent on vengeance for past wrongs. He invades their lives, exposing their most intimate secrets and lies.

"The secret to eternal youth—as One Last Dance *shows with eloquence, grace, and unsentimental wit—isn't exercise or Lipitor but falling in love—and it's never too late."* —**Ralph Gardner, Jr.,** *The New York Observer*

Mardo Williams completed the first draft of this novel at age 95, after a distinguished career as journalist and author—for which he won an Ohioana Library Award. He asked his daughters Kay and Jerri (both writers) to finish the book if he could not. He died a few weeks later. His daughters honored their father's wishes.

Topics for Discussion

1. In the novel, Dixie is 79 and Morgan is 89. How realistic is it to expect to fall in love at that age? Discuss the complications of romance and marriage at this stage in life. Also talk about the advantages.

2. Dixie would possibly like a relationship but does not want to turn into a caregiver. Do you think she is selfish? Would you take the kind of risk she takes by inviting Morgan into her life? Discuss your thoughts about whether women manage being alone better than men do.

3. Dixie has concerns regarding Morgan's past. Is she right to be worried? Has Morgan been treated fairly by his family? Did he create some of his own problems? Grandson Tony has been led to believe that his Grandpa is wealthy. How do Tony's family, friends and the people he meets in Columbus influence Tony's outlook and attitude? Discuss how Officer Pfeiffer handles Tony. How does Tony impact the lives of Dixie and Morgan?

4. In the story, Dixie struggles to keep her house up and considers taking in a boarder. For retirees, finances can be a huge issue even with the best of planning. The thought of losing independence is painful. Moving to a retirement home means giving up privacy and independence for the rest of life. The novel also touches on end-of-life choices. How do we prepare to face these difficult decisions?

5. After the accident, Morgan's recovery is slow—in part due to his age. Dixie ends up being the caregiver after all and cannot go to her job even though she has bills to pay and needs the money. Morgan ends up in Whispering Pines Nursing Home and Dixie must face the cold hard facts of Medicare and Medicaid and the sad cost of being old and sick in America. Are there solutions to these problems? Do you have hope that they'll be implemented for your benefit?

6. Morgan thinks to himself, "Who would ever believe the best thing that ever happened to me happened at age 90!" Do you think the same is possible in your own life?

7. The author, Mardo Williams, wrote his first novel at age 92. He suggests we live life every minute and always be in search of new experiences regardless of age. Discuss the title of the book and how it fits the story. How did the novel influence your thoughts and expectations for the future?

THE OUTSIDE WORLD

Author: *Tova Mirvis*

Publisher: Vintage Books, 2005

Web site: www.readinggroupcenter.com

Available in:
Paperback, 304 pages. $13.00
ISBN 1-4000-7528-9

Subject: Family Life/Jewish Interest
(Fiction)

Summary: Tzippy Goldman was born for marriage. She and her mother had always assumed she'd graduate high school, be set up with the right boy, and have a beautiful wedding. But at twenty-two, Tzippy's fast approaching spinsterhood. She dreams of escape; instead, she leaves for a year in Jerusalem. There she meets—remeets—Baruch, the son of her mother's college roommate. When Tzippy last saw him, his name was Bryan and he wore a Yankees-logo yarmulke. Now he has adopted the black hat of the ultra-Orthodox, the tradition in which Tzippy was raised. Twelve weeks later, they're engaged . . . and discovering that achieving a balance between desire and tradition, devotion and individuality isn't so easy to do.

"A brilliant evocation of Orthodox life. . . . Beneath the women's wigs and the men's black fedora's, Mirvis finds reservoirs of belief, doubt, ambition, folly, lust and the rest of the human equation."
—**The Washington Post Book World**

Tova Mirvis grew up in Memphis, Tennessee. She received an MFA in creative writing from Columbia University. She lives outside of Boston with her husband and two children. She can be found online at www.tovamirvis.com.

Topics for Discussion

1. How does Bryan/Baruch's return from Israel change the life of the Miller family? What reactions does he provoke in his father and his sister? When one family member becomes a strict interpreter of the religion that the entire family practices, is he a tyrant or a reformer?

2. Who is the ideal or intended audience of this novel? Does it seem that Mirvis wants to create a view of this closed community for the outside world or show the Orthodox community a reflection of itself? How do the ideas she explores in the novel about belonging and not belonging, feeling trapped or stifled by one's family, and the yearning for authentic spirituality move beyond the particular community that she describes?

3. When we meet Tzippy, she is simultaneously dreaming of rebellion against her mother and raging against her unmarried fate. As the novel ends, she is married and pregnant. She hasn't stepped outside the role for which her family prepared her, but she has changed. How is she different? Does the novel suggest that she will live life on her own terms, within the parameters of Orthodoxy, and that she and Baruch will forge a better partnership than her own parents did?

4. How does the novel show the distance between the women's and men's spheres of responsibility in the Orthodox community? Why are the ways of the household, cooking, and child-rearing so crucial to passing on the Orthodox way of life? What aspects of Orthodox life, as described in the novel, might present the most difficult challenges to an educated woman?

5. Why is Naomi driven to take such an active role in seeking meaning and answers in her life? What does she expect to find in books, meditation, and seminars on Jewish spirituality? What is admirable about her as a character?

6. Does the ending of the novel suggest that Tzippy will take an active role in healing her own family's troubles—her mother's despondency, her father's dangerously unrealistic dreams, her unguided little sisters? Or will she return to Memphis and take up her own family life, keeping a distance from her difficult parents?

For a complete Reading Group Guide, visit www.readinggroupcenter.com

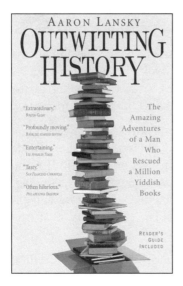

OUTWITTING HISTORY

Author: *Aaron Lansky*

Publisher: Algonquin Books
of Chapel Hill, 2005

Website: www.algonquin.com

Available in:
Paperback, 328 pages. $13.95
ISBN 1-56512-513-4
Hardcover, 328 pages. $24.95 (2004)
ISBN 1-56512-429-4

Subject: Memoir/History (Nonfiction)

Summary: In 1980, a twenty-three-year-old graduate student named Aaron Lansky set out to rescue the world's abandoned Yiddish books before it was too late. Twenty-five years and one and a half million books later, he's still in the midst of a great adventure. Filled with poignant and often laugh-out-loud tales from Lansky's travels across the country collecting books from older Jewish immigrants, *Outwitting History* also introduces us to a dazzling array of writers and shows us how an almost-lost culture is the bridge between the old world and the future.

"A marvelous yarn, loaded with near-calamitous adventures and characters as memorable as Singer creations."—New York Post

"What began as a quixotic journey was also a picaresque romp, a detective story, a profound history lesson, and a poignant evocation of a bygone world. Lansky's extraordinary storytelling conveys the daunting task he set for himself."—The Boston Sunday Globe

"A rollicking ride in company with a man who has performed an enormously important public service."—Kirkus Reviews, starred review

"Hilarious and moving."—Publishers Weekly, starred review

Aaron Lansky is the founder and president of the National Yiddish Book Center (www.yiddishbookcenter.org) in Amherst, Massachusetts. The recipient of a MacArthur "genius" fellowship, Lansky has helped fuel a renaissance of Jewish literature in this country. He lives with his family in western Massachusetts.

Topics for Discussion

1. The humorous scene that follows lunch at the Garden Cafeteria highlights the central theme of difference and similarity developed throughout the book. How does difference yield to common cause at the physical level and the emotional level in this vignette?

2. Characters in this story are dressed in particular and significant ways. How do the clothes help us to understand people, priorities, and cultures in *Outwitting History*?

3. What do books mean to Lansky and to the people who donate them? Why did books take on such special importance for Jewish immigrants in America? Do books bear meaning in your family or cultural history?

4. Why did so many older Jews consider their Yiddish books their *yerushe* or "inheritance"? How is this concept of inheritance different from or similar to your own?

5. The differences of the Hebrew and Aramaic books and that of the Yiddish books are those of classical and popular culture, of high and low art. How do those distinctions play out in the book? How do other distinctions between high and low culture affect your life?

6. Discuss some of the ways the next generation considered themselves to be "unlike" their immigrant grandparents. Is it unusual to find children more interested in the generation of their grandparents than that of their parents?

7. Lansky describes the National Yiddish Book Center as a "home" for Yiddish books. Why did these books need a "home"? What motivated Lansky's choice of Amherst, Massachusetts for the National Yiddish Book Center?

8. What opposition to a National Yiddish Book Center did Lansky encounter and have to overcome? What were the political and fiscal realities with which he grappled?

9. What does Lansky mean when he describes the Canadian immigration experience as a "mosaic" rather than a melting pot? How did American Jewish culture and Canadian Jewish culture develop differently?

10. Who is your favorite hero or what is your favorite vignette from the book? How does this personal story fit into the larger historical context?

11. In the end, do you think Yiddish "outwits" history? Why or why not?

THE PLOT AGAINST AMERICA

Author: *Philip Roth*

Publisher: Vintage Books, 2005

Web site: www.readinggroupcenter.com

Available in:
Paperback, 416 pages. $14.95
ISBN 1-4000-7949-7

Subject: American Culture/ Identity/
Family Life (Fiction)

Summary: In an astonishing feat of empathy and narrative invention, our most ambitious novelist imagines an alternate version of American history. In 1940 Charles A. Lindbergh, heroic aviator and rabid isolationist, is elected president. Shortly thereafter, he negotiates a cordial "understanding" with Adolf Hitler, while the new government embarks on a program of folksy anti-Semitism. For one boy growing up in Newark, New Jersey, Lindbergh's election is the first in a series of ruptures that threaten to destroy his small, safe corner of America—and with it, his mother, his father, and his older brother.

"A terrific political novel . . . sinister, vivid, dreamlike . . . creepily plausible. . . . You turn the pages, astonished and frightened."
—The New York Times Book Review

In 1997, **Philip Roth** won the Pulitzer Prize for *American Pastoral*. In 1998 he received the National Medal of Arts at the White House, and in 2002 received the highest award of the American Academy of Arts and Letters, the Gold Medal in Fiction, previously awarded to John Dos Passos, William Faulkner, and Saul Bellow, among others. He has twice won the National Book Award, the PEN/Faulkner Award, and the National Book Critics Circle Award.

Topics for Discussion

1. In what ways does *The Plot Against America* differ from conventional historical fiction? What effects does Roth achieve by blending personal history, historical fact, and an alternative history?

2. The novel begins "Fear presides over these memories, a perpetual fear." With this sentence Roth establishes that his story is being told from an adult point of view by an adult narrator who is remembering what befell his family, over sixty years earlier, when he was a boy between the ages of seven and nine. Why else does Roth open the novel this way? What role does fear play throughout the book?

3. Herman Roth asserts, "History is everything that happens everywhere. Even here in Newark. Even here on Summit Avenue. Even what happens in this house to an ordinary man—that'll be history too someday." How does this conception of history differ from traditional definitions? In what ways does the novel support this claim? How is the history of the Roth family relevant to the history of America?

4. Observing his mother's anguished confusion, Philip discovers that "one could do nothing right without also doing something wrong." Where in the novel does the attempt to do something right also result in doing something wrong? What is Roth suggesting here about the moral complexities of actions and their consequences?

5. When Herman Roth is explaining the deals Hitler has made with Lindbergh, Roth comments, "The pressure of what was happening was accelerating everyone's education, my own included." What is Philip learning? In what ways is history robbing him of a normal childhood? Why does he want to run away?

6. Much is at stake in *The Plot Against America*—the fate of America's Jews, the larger fate of Europe and indeed of Western civilization, but also how America will define itself. What does the novel suggest about what it means to be an American, and to be a Jewish American? How are the Roths a thoroughly American family?

For a complete Reading Group Guide and to read a note from the author, visit www.readinggroupcenter.com

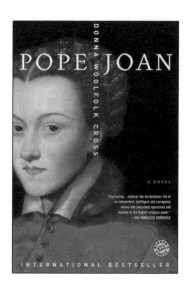

POPE JOAN

Author: *Donna Woolfolk Cross*

Publisher: Ballantine Books, 2005

Website: www.popejoan.com

Available in:
Quality paperback, 422 pages. $14.95
ISBN 0-345-41626-0

Subject: Women's Issues/Women's
Lives/Women's Studies/History/Personal
Challenges/Personal Triumphs/Identity/
Cultural and World Issues (Fiction)

Summary: For more than a millennium, her existence has been hidden and denied. But hers is the legend that will not die—Pope Joan, the woman who, disguised as a man, rose to rule Christianity in the ninth century as the one and only woman ever to sit on the Throne of St. Peter.

In this stirring international bestseller, Donna Woolfolk Cross brings the Dark Ages to life in all their brutal splendor, and shares the dramatic story of a woman who struggles against restrictions her soul cannot accept—a woman whose courage makes her a heroine for every age.

Soon to be a major motion picture.

"A fascinating and moving account of a woman's determination to learn despite the opposition of family and society. . . . Cross vividly creates the 9th century world. . . . Above all, she brings to life a brilliant, compassionate woman who has to deny her gender to satisfy her desire for learning. Highly recommended." —Library Journal

Donna Woolfolk Cross is the author of *Word Abuse* and *Mediaspeak*, two books on language. The product of seven years of research and writing, *Pope Joan* is her first novel. Cross is at work on a new novel set in 17th century France.

Topics for Discussion

1. Did Joan make the right choice at that moment when she decided to disguise herself as her dead brother? What would her life have been like had she chosen differently?

2. What happens to Joan when she tries to improve the lives of women and the poor? Why do you think Church and civic leaders were resistant to such improvements? Have there been similar instances in modern society?

3. Discuss the inner conflicts Joan faces. How do these conflicts affect the decisions she makes? Are they ever truly resolved?

4. Do you think Joan's secret would ever have been discovered had she not miscarried during the Papal procession or had she not become pregnant?

5. If the Viking raid had not intervened to keep them apart, do you think Joan and Gerold could have had a happy life together?

6. Why do you think medieval society considered it unnatural and a sin for women to educate themselves or be educated? It was also believed that education hampered a woman's ability to bear children. What purpose might that belief have served?

7. Although the position of women in society has changed dramatically since the middle ages, do you feel there are similarities between the way women live in various societies today and the way they lived in society then?

8. According to one reviewer, "Joan has the kind of vices—stubbornness and outspokenness, for example—that turn out to be virtues." Do you agree? If so, why? If not, why not?

9. How important is it that Pope Joan actually existed? Are there lessons to be learned from this story whether it's true or not? What do you think those lessons are?

ROMANCING THE BUDDHA
Embracing Buddhism in My Everyday Life

Author: *Michael Lisagor*

Publisher: Middleway Press, 2005

Website: www.middlewaypress.com

Available in:
Paperback, 177 pages. $14.00
ISBN 0-9723267-4-X

Subject: Buddhism/Marriage/Parenting
(Nonfiction)

Summary: Join Michael Lisagor on his hunt for lost treasure in the jungles of urban America and the depths of his life, as he transforms from a confused and sad teenager into a creative and happy adult, father and spouse. With warmth and wit, Lisagor chronicles his thirty-six years of applying Buddhist practice and principles to his life.

Gain a better understanding of Nichiren Buddhism, learn how to apply Buddhist principles to your life, raise happy children, overcome major challenges and build successful, loving relationships with *Romancing the Buddha*. The book also contains an overview of Nichiren Buddhism as well as a glossary of Buddhist terms.

"Romancing the Buddha *is a wise and moving account of the author's adventuresome journey toward spiritual enlightenment and social awareness. Michael Lisagor's work helps us to understand the intimate connection between resolving conflicts in one's personal life and working effectively for peace on a global scale.* —**Richard E. Rubenstein, Professor of Conflict Resolution, George Mason University**

Michael Lisagor is happily married with two grown daughters. A long-time contributor to the Buddhist publications *World Tribune* and *Living Buddhism*, he also writes a regular column for *Federal Computer Week* magazine. A resident of Bainbridge Island, Washington, he is the president of Celerity Works, a management consulting company.

Topics for Discussion

1. How does the Prologue prepare you for what's ahead in the book? Discuss his choice of words in the introductory sentence.

2. Lisagor uses personal stories to talk about faith, everyday life and happiness. Were there particular stories that had special value to you?

3. Throughout the book, Lisagor refers to his wife, Trude, as "Most Beautiful One." Discuss what you learned about their marriage from reading the book, how the relationship has changed over time and what has made this marriage last.

4. "The Early Morning Blues" is about learning to get up early—and liking it. How does one develop the ability to reframe—or take a different view of—something that at first seems negative in our lives? How might familiarity with Buddhist teachings affect the ability to reframe any situation?

5. Lisagor ends the chapter on "Thoughts on Marriage" by claiming that, "It's important to romance the Buddha not just in ourselves but in those around us." What does this mean to you how does it apply to your own life and your relationship with others?

6. In discussing young people in "Teenagers Are Aliens," Lisagor suggests, "To be effective, a religion must not be so restrictive that it refuses to encourage a respect for diversity and open mindedness in young people." What dynamics are at work today in our culture that influence young people either directly or through role models? What trends do you see?

7. What is it about the nature of chanting Nam-myoho-renge-kyo that helps affect change? How can a single individual's efforts affect the global community?

8. Lisagor states that for him, "The most meaningful benefit I can have in my life is the satisfaction that, yes, I am progressing as a human being." Can you relate?

9. Discuss your thoughts about the December holiday celebrations at the Lisagor household as described in the chapter "Holiday Identity Crisis." Have you faced a similar dilemma in your life?

10. Lisagor chooses an essay on happiness as his last of the book. How does your vision of happiness match that of the author's? How would you describe the feeling you'd like to have on your last day in this lifetime?

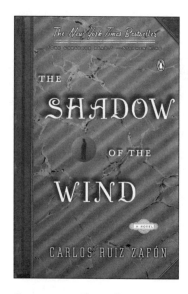

THE SHADOW OF THE WIND

Author: *Carlos Ruiz Zafón*

Translated by: Lucia Graves

Publisher: Penguin, 2005

Website: www.penguin.com

Available in:
Paperback, 496 pages. $15.00
ISBN 0-14-303490-1

Subject: Suspense/Thriller/Love/
Books and Reading (Fiction)

Summary: Barcelona, 1945—A great world city lies shrouded in secrets after the war, and a boy mourning the loss of his mother finds solace in his love for an extraordinary book called *The Shadow of the Wind,* by an author named Julian Carax. When the boy searches for Carax's other books, it begins to dawn on him, to his horror, that someone has been systematically destroying every copy of every book the man has ever written. Soon the boy realizes that *The Shadow of the Wind* is as dangerous to own as it is impossible to forget, for the mystery of its author's identity holds the key to an epic story of murder, madness, and doomed love that someone will go to any lengths to keep secret.

"If you thought the true gothic novel died with the nineteenth century, this will change your mind. . . . This is one gorgeous read." —**Stephen King**

"Anyone who enjoys novels that are scary, erotic, touching, tragic and thrilling should rush right out . . . and pick up The Shadow of the Wind.*"*
—**Michael Dirda,** *The Washington Post*

Carlos Ruiz Zafón lives in Barcelona with his wife. Lucia Graves is the author and translator of many works and has overseen Spanish-language editions of the poetry of her father, Robert Graves.

Topics for Discussion

1. Julián Carax's and Daniel's lives follow very similar trajectories. Yet one ends in tragedy, the other in happiness. What similarities are there between the paths they take? What are the differences that allow Daniel to avoid tragedy?

2. Nuria Monfort tells Daniel, "Julián once wrote that coincidences are the scars of fate. There are no coincidences, Daniel. We are the puppets of our unconscious." What does that mean? What does she refer to in her own experience and in Julián's life?

3. Nuria Monfort's dying words, meant for Julián, are, "There are worse prisons than words." What does she mean by this? What is she referring to?

4. There are many devil figures in the story—Carax's Laín Coubert, Jacinta's Zacarias, Fermín's Fumero. How does evil manifest itself in each devil figure? What are the characteristics of the villains/devils?

5. What is "The Shadow of the Wind"? Where does Zafón refer to it and what does he use the image to illustrate?

6. Zafón's female characters are often enigmatic, otherworldly angels full of power and mystery. Do you think Zafón paints his female characters differently than his male characters? What do the women represent in Daniel's life? What might the Freud loving Miquel Moliner say about Daniel's relationships with women?

7. Daniel says of *The Shadow of the Wind,* "As it unfolded, the structure of the story began to remind me of one of those Russian dolls that contain innumerable ever-smaller dolls within." Zafón's *The Shadow of the Wind* unfolds much the same way, with many characters contributing fragments of their own stories in the first person point of view. What does Zafón illustrate with this method of storytelling? What do the individual mini-autobiographies contribute to the tale?

8. The evil Fumero is the only son of a ridiculed father and a superficial, status-seeking mother. The troubled Julián is the bastard son of a love-starved musical mother and an amorous, amoral businessman, though he was raised by a cuckolded hatmaker. Do you think their personalities are products of nature or nurture? How are the sins of the fathers and mothers visited upon each of the characters?

SHADOWS IN THE ASYLUM

Author: *D.A. Stern*

Publisher: Emmis Books
January 2006

Website: www.emmisbooks.com

Available in:
Paperback, 224 pages. $14.95
ISBN 1-57860-204-1

Subject: Paranormal (Fiction)

Summary:

In the tradition of H.P. Lovecraft.
In the style of Griffin and Sabine.
In the woods of Northern Wisconsin . . .
A terrible darkness stirs.

Dr. Charles Marsh arrives at the Kriegmoor Psychiatric Institute in Bayfield Wisconsin, eager to take on his new duties as a means of distancing himself from a scandal that erupted at his previous post in Texas.

During Marsh's first days at the Institute, he is assigned the case of Kari Hansen, a young girl teetering on the edge of madness, haunted by visions of shadows that only she can see.

Yet as he begins to treat her, Marsh makes a series of startling discoveries—parallels between the figures tormenting Kari and legends of the Native American tribes that once inhabited Bayield—connections between her visions, and the fluid nature of reality, as espoused in the writings of reclusive scientist Raymond Laszlo—similarities between Kari's breakdown and the mysterious disappearance of 1960s teen idol Danny Rasmussen—all of which lead Marsh to a final, fateful conclusion . . .

The shadows are real.
And only he can stop them.

D.A. Stern lives in Northampton Massachusetts. He is the author of multiple works of fiction and non-fiction, including *The Blair Witch Project: A Dossier* and *Your Secrets Are My Business*.

Topics for Discussion

1. Do you believe in the supernatural? Did reading this book change any of your beliefs? If so, how?

2. Do you think science will eventually find an explanation for every inexplicable/supernatural phenomenon?

3. Discuss how Kari Hansen was treated as a patient by the doctors at Kriegmoor. Consider, in particular, her treatment by Dr. Marsh versus her treatment by Dr. Ferguson. Contrast with your own experiences, either as a patient or, as in the case of Kari's mother, as a member of the family or friend of a patient.

4. Do you think the creatures Dr. Marsh encountered were real or his imagination?

5. How do you feel about the death penalty? Does the possibility that there is an afterlife influence those feelings?

6. Did you like experiencing the story through the mechanism of 'found documents,' as opposed to a traditional text narrative? What was good/bad about this storytelling method? What do you see as its strengths/weaknesses?

7. How do you feel about religion? Do you see it as Dr. Marsh did, as an attempt by primitive man to explain aspects of the natural world he could not understand?

8. What is the single action you've taken in your life you feel most guilty about?

9. Are there places you've visited that carried a foreboding feeling, as if previous generations somehow still had an influence or control?

10. Considering the various ways that characters were "opened up" to see the shadows—by illness, isolation, drugs—do you believe there are parts of our senses rationally closed off to other phenomena in life? If so, what else do you think is out there?

11. For earlier or indigenous civilizations not based in current religious beliefs, do you think the culture and practices and vengeances of these peoples still affect our world?

12. If there are spirits among us, vestiges of people and willful actions from long ago, do you think we can change or communicate with them?

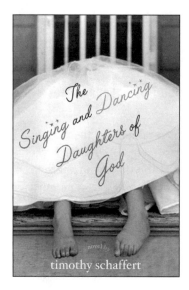

THE SINGING AND DANCING DAUGHTERS OF GOD

Author: *Timothy Schaffert*

Publisher: Unbridled Books, 2005

Website: www.unbridledbooks.com

Available in:
Paperback, 256 pages. $14.95
ISBN 1-932961-12-7

Subject: Family/Music (Fiction)

Summary: Newly divorced and feeling the pain of separation from his family, Hud Smith channels his regret into writing country-western songs, contemplating life on the lam with his 8-year-old daughter, and searching cryptic postcards for news of his teenage son, who has run off with The Daughters of God, an alternative Gospel-punk band of growing fame.

In this endearing misadventure that threatens to turn out right in spite of it all, Schaffert writes a thin line between tragedy and hilarity, turning wry humor and a keen sense of the paradoxical onto characters who deserve all the tender care he gives them.

*"Achy-breaky dysfunction drives a messy, funny family drama in this smalltown Nebraska tale, told in a winning faux-naïve style . . . film, along with music, plays a wonderful incidental role throughout. . . . Deft, sweet and surprising." —***Publishers Weekly**

Timothy Schaffert grew up on a farm in Nebraska and currently lives in Omaha. He's the author of the critically acclaimed novel, *The Phantom Limbs of the Rollow Sisters*. His short fiction has been published in several literary journals and he's won numerous awards, including the Mary Roberts Rinehart Award and the Nebraska Book Award.

Topics for Discussion

1. What will become of Hud and Tuesday's relationship, following their adventure to South Dakota?

2. Discuss the theme of fight/flight throughout Hud and Tuesday's relationship, both in their direct interactions with each other, and their interactions through their children.

3. How is Hud's relationship to music, and the writing of songs, different from that of Gatling's?

4. How does church and religion inform the characters' lives? In what do the characters have the greatest faith?

5. What affect do the movies have on the characters' sense of romance? How do movies affect their senses of themselves?

6. What role does Halloween play in this novel, and why do you think the author featured this holiday rather than another?

7. How are children both treasured and protected, or not, in this novel?

8. The book begins with Hud's ruminations about how society comes together over tragedy, grief, and loss. Is this book a tragedy, a comedy, or both?

9. How did Hud's and Tuesday's marrying young affect their lives and inform their regrets? What is their sense of family and sense of community, and how does this play out both in the family break up and in their hopes for reuniting?

10. Why do you think the author chose such distinctive names for his characters? How do the names develop the characters for readers?

11. How do Hud's and Tuesday's youthful expectations for moving beyond the limitations of their town color their sense of the future, their attitudes about their marriage, and their relationships with their children?

12. How much of their nostalgia for a better time is genuine and how does it affect their dreams for a future?

13. What role does music play in this novel?

14. Is this a love story? If so, whose?

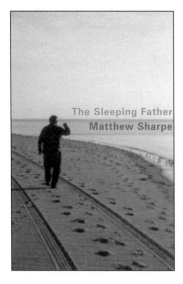

THE SLEEPING FATHER

Author: *Matthew Sharpe*

Publisher: Soft Skull Press, 2003

Website: www.softskull.com

Available in:
Paperback, 291 pages. $14.00
ISBN 1-932360-00-X

Subject: Divorce/Race Relations/
Religion/Mental Health/Jewish Families/
Suburbs (Fiction)

Summary: Bernard Schwartz has lost his wife, his career, and finally, thanks to the accidental combination of two classes of antidepressants, his consciousness. He emerges from a coma to find his son Chris, the perpetual smart-ass, and his daughter Cathy, a Jewish teen turned self-martyred Catholic, stumbling headlong toward trauma-induced maturity. *The Sleeping Father* is about the loss of innocence, the disorienting innocence of second childhood, the biochemical mechanics of sanity and love, the nature of language and meaning, and the spirituality of selfhood. But most of all it is about the Schwartzes, a typical American family making their way the best way they know how in a small town called Bellwether, Connecticut.

"This novel is fluent and funny, clever and wise. It is so skillfully constructed and its tempo so beautifully modulated that it slowly becomes sad without you noticing and then frightening and then funny again. In The Sleeping Father, *Matthew Sharpe proves himself a master conjuror of tones.*—**Colm Toibin, author of *The Master***

February 2004 TODAY SHOW Book Club Pick, and selected for the *New York Times Book Review's* Summer 2004 Reading List

Matthew Sharpe is the author of the novel *Nothing Is Terrible* and the short-story collection *Stories from the Tube.* He teaches creative writing at Columbia University, Bard College, and in New York City public schools. His stories and essays have appeared in *Harper's, Zoetrope, BOMB, American Letters & Commentary, Southwest Review,* and *Teachers & Writers* magazine.

Topics for Discussion

1. Why do you think the author called his novel *The Sleeping Father*? Does the title have any significance beyond the fact that Bernard Schwartz falls into a coma?

2. How does the novel treat the questions of race, class, and religion in Bellwether, Connecticut? How does Bellwether differ from neighboring Port Town? How do the differences affect the lives of Cathy and Chris Schwartz?

3. Do you find the novel funny? Painful? Both of these? Neither? Why?

4. One reviewer has described *The Sleeping Father* as a "stylistically thrilling inquiry into the weight of words" (Ed Park, *Village Voice*, March 3–9, 2004). Can you find passages in the book that illustrate this point? Do you agree with this critic's judgment?

5. Describe the relationship between the father, Bernard Schwartz, and his son, Chris. What are its positive and negative qualities?

6. What does Cathy, a Jewish girl, seek in Catholicism? How much of her quest is due to her personality, and how much to the larger issues of religious faith?

7. How would you describe the friendship between the white Chris Schwartz and the African-American Frank Dial? What are its positive aspects? What are its tensions? What role does their mutual love of language play in their friendship? How do the actions of the bully Robert Stone affect their relationship?

8. How would you describe Bernard Schwartz's personality before and after his illness? What kind of person is Lila Schwartz? What does she learn from her relationship with Moe Danmeyer?

9. How does the Schwartz's divorce affect their children? Do Chris and Cathy succeed in resolving their relationships to their father and mother?

10. What does Chris think of Dr. Lisa Danmeyer? How does Dr. Danmeyer react to Chris's behavior? What contradictions does she experience in her role as a doctor?

11. How does Chris try to cope with the pain and difficulty of his life? What part does irony play in his attitude? How does he differ from his sister Cathy? How are they alike?

SOMEONE NOT REALLY HER MOTHER

Author: *Harriet Scott Chessman*

Publisher: Plume Books, 2005

Websites: www.penguin.com
www.HarrietChessman.com

Available in:
Paperback, 176 pages. $13.00
ISBN 0-452-28697-2

Subject: Family Relationships/
Jewish Studies/Alzheimers (Fiction)

Summary: As dementia overtakes Hannah Pearl, she slips backward in memory to her escape from France in 1940; boarding the ferry with her heavy bags; the whistle of bombs raining down on London; the family she left behind. Her daughter Miranda, distraught by Hannah's fading lucidity and sudden switch to her childhood French, tries desperately to hold her in the present. Fiona, a new mother and the older of Hannah's two granddaughters, ignores the ghosts of her grandmother's past, while her sister, fiery Ida, seeks to delve into Hannah's story, eventually returning to France to find the roots of her grandmother's life—and her own.

A *Good Morning America* "Read This" Book Club pick

Harriet Scott Chessman is the author of *Lydia Cassatt Reading the Morning Paper*. Formerly associate professor of English at Yale University, Chessman has also taught literature and writing at Bread Loaf School of English and Wesleyan University, and has published several essays on modern literature. She lives in the Bay Area with her family.

Topics for Discussion

1. The title *Someone Not Really Her Mother* implies a number of meanings. How do you interpret it?

2. How does Hannah Pearl's loss of memory and inability to find the right words enhance the narrative? How does language play a crucial role in this novel?

3. We see through Hannah how the trauma experienced by the generation who grew up during the Second World War affected the second and third generations. How has Miranda been affected by her mother's past? Ida and Fiona have also been affected by their grandmother's past but in different ways. How do you explain these differences?

4. On page 109, Hannah says, "Je suis tellement desolee," and this feeling of being so very sorry, too sorry for words fills this bright air now . . ." Why does Hannah feel so sorry?

5. Harriet Chessman's novel is filled with wonderful imagery. For example, on page 3, we are told that Hannah Pearl notices a "young woman with hair the color of honey," echoing the image of the bee in the quote by Virginia Woolf, given in the beginning of the novel. This image is picked up again on page 15, when Hannah remembers another girl with hair "The color of honey," and remembers that this girl is Miranda. Why is imagery so important in this novel? Can you find any other significant images?

6. Do you agree with Miranda when she says, "Could it be that her mother's deepest sorrow is about something more even than the invasion by the Germans, or the Occupation, or what came after? That it's about something in addition to the history she had to breathe and move in, day to day, minute to minute—something in addition to her grievous loss? Could it be that, at the core, it's a question of love? Could it be this ordinary a logic, yet misguided? Emma was kept, proving that Emma was loved. Hannah was sent to England, proving that Hannah was not loved."

7. Why is it significant that Hannah Pearl now speaks French after not speaking it for so many years?

8. The novel ends with Hannah and her grandson, Seamus. Why is this the perfect place to end the novel?

For complete reading group guide, visit www.penguin.com.

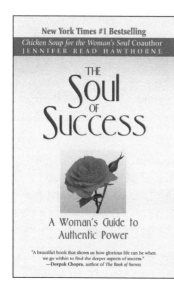

New York Times #1 Bestselling
Chicken Soup for the Woman's Soul Coauthor
JENNIFER READ HAWTHORNE

THE
Soul
OF
Success

A Woman's Guide to
Authentic Power

"A beautiful book that shows us how glorious life can be when
we go within to find the deeper aspects of success."
—Deepak Chopra, author of *The Book of Secrets*

THE SOUL OF SUCCESS
A Woman's Guide to Authentic Power

Author: *Jennifer Read Hawthorne*

Publisher: Health Communications, Inc., 2005

Website: www.hcibooks.com

Available in:
Paperback, 300 pages. $12.95
ISBN 0-7573-0236-X

Subject: Women's Issues/Self-Help/ Inspiration (Nonfiction)

Summary: The quest for success has left many women struggling to find balance in life. This book shows how the author and 27 women from many walks of life broke through to a deeper experience of success in their personal and professional lives by tapping into their authentic power. Through their moving personal stories, the book explores the principles that enabled them to embrace challenge and transformation: Ginny Walden beat breast cancer through self-love; Catherine Oxenberg overcame bulimia through receptivity; Catherine Carter dealt with the discovery that her husband was gay through acceptance; corporate VP Jacqui Vines got very honest about her life and took on the raising of two small children; grace enabled Nancy Bellmer and her husband to stay married after he accidentally killed their young son. These and other stories illustrate 27 essential principles of authenticity, including commitment, openness, forgiveness and compassion, that will serve as guideposts to a more meaningful life.

"The Soul of Success *encompasses everything I believe in. Integrity, faith, honesty, intuition and courage are traits that we all have, yet we sometimes forget to trust and believe in them. Trusting in your soul is the key to your success. Well written and worth the read.*" — **Erin Brockovich**

Jennifer Read Hawthorne is an inspirational speaker and award-winning co-author of the #1 *New York Times* best-sellers *Chicken Soup for the Woman's Soul* and *Chicken Soup for the Mother's Soul.*

Topics for Discussion

1. Which stories resonated most deeply with you? Did you see yourself in any of the women? What principles may be key areas of growth for you?

2. Women's intuition is prized, but have we lost touch with it? Discuss Lynne Twist's experience with the African women who intuited the presence of water. Do we have comparable ability latent within us? Are there ways we can strengthen our intuition?

3. Is achieving material success a high priority for you? What expectations do you have about how it will benefit your life? If you've had material gains thus far, have they increased your freedom? Discuss Despina Gurlides's experience.

4. Is there a chance that self-doubt and fear of failure are masking your true desires? Alexis Quinlan discovered she had been avoiding the truth about what she wanted and her responsibility to create it. In what ways can we be more accountable to ourselves?

5. Every person is born with a special natural ability. What were you drawn to as a child, and are you expressing it, either at work or play? Do you discount your gift because it comes easily to you?

6. Catherine Oxenberg's life was transformed by a dream she had. Do you believe dreams can give us knowledge or helpful insights? Are there other sources of wisdom and support we could access if we were more receptive to them?

7. In the light of 9/11, Jacqui Vines rethought her priorities and values and made a profound change in her life. Has there been a point in your life when you made a major shift? What were the results?

8. Discuss Susan Brandis Slavin's relationship with her sister. How do mental health problems complicate family relationships and issues of guilt, responsibility and forgiveness?

9. Nancy Bellmer and Catherine Carter both found peace in the face of profound challenge. Discuss how marriages are affected by losses and life changes. What makes a marriage survive or not? What role does grace play in our dealing with tragedy?

10. Authenticity means living your life so that everything on the outside lines up with who you are on the inside. This is also what it means to be "true to yourself." What's true for you at this point in your life, and does your life reflect who you are on the inside?

For a complete Reader's Guide, visit www.thesoulofsuccess.com

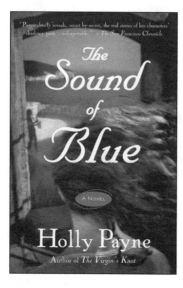

THE SOUND OF BLUE

Author: *Holly Payne*

Publisher: Plume Books, 2005

Website: www.penguin.com
www.Holly-Payne.com

Available in:
Paperback, 336 pages. $14.00
ISBN 0-452-28698-0

Subject: Personal Discovery/
European History/Travel (Fiction)

Summary: Sara Foster has left America for the adventure of lifetime—teaching English to the sons and daughters of statesmen in Hungary—but her idyllic adventure instead reveals a dark world of pain and redemption when she ends up teaching in a refugee camp. Sara discovers that one of her students is a celebrated composer and soon finds herself crossing the border to his war-torn homeland, determined to exonerate him for the death of his brother.

In a journey that takes her to Dubrovnik, a magnificent stone city on the Croatian Riviera, Sara contemplates her own identity, struggling to understand why the region's ancient and extraordinary beauty belies a history of grief. As Sara unveils the secret of the composer's escape, *The Sound of Blue* reveals poignant truths about the quests for refuge we all pursue.

"Payne slowly reveals, secret by secret, the real stories of her characters' shadowy pasts . . . unforgettable." —San Francisco Chronicle

Holly Payne has traveled extensively throughout Turkey and Croatia and lived in southern Hungary for a year, where much of *The Sound of Blue* takes place. She holds an MFA from the Master of Professional Writing Program at USC and teaches screenwriting and creative writing at the Academy of Art University in San Francisco.

Topics for Discussion

1. The novel begins with Sara's startling arrival in a refugee camp where she meets a Red Cross nurse who warns her about the implications of befriending the refugees. "The minute you open your heart to a refugee, you suffer everything they have suffered and more." How is the reverse of this warning significant to the point of the novel?

2. Bridges and silence function in tandem as recurring motifs and images in this story. What do the bridges of "Sokhid" (Town of Many Bridges) symbolize for the refugees and for Sara? How many 'movie moments' do you recall with bridges in both Sokhid and in Dubrovnik?

3. When Sara arrives in Croatia, she meets the director of the refugee camp. Gabor takes a liking to Sara and immediately brings her into the fold of life at the camp, trying to impress her. Why does Sara feel that she cannot accept his gifts? Why does she harbor guilt?

4. Gabor is a complicated character in that he is part buffoon, part villain. He is a shape shifting character who serves as both an ally and an enemy to Sara. In what ways does Gabor resent his job as the director of the refugee camp? How have the politics of post-communism Hungary affected his morality?

5. Luka, like most children his age at the brink of the war, had never seen tanks or snipers. Luka only hears of sniper nests on the radio news and mistakes snipers for birds. What is the irony of his thinking, "why somebody didn't shoot the birds if they were so scary?"

6. Dubrovnik has always been known for its diplomacy and the quality of its orphanages, having established one of Europe's first in the old town nunnery. In the novel, the nuns and monks of Dubrovnik have been searching for Luka for months, determined to capture him and offer him a place in the orphanages. Why does Luka refuse to enter the orphanage?

7. Milan's composition *The Sound of Blue* is an expression of civil war. Discuss the nature of the "civil war" between Milan and his half-brother, Damir. What are the eerie similarities between that conflict and the one between Sara and her cousin Mark?

8. Discuss the significance of Luka's standing on the gargoyle, against the wall, in the final scene. How is the boy's courage and faith rewarded despite the trauma he suffered?

For complete reading group guide, visit www.penguin.com.

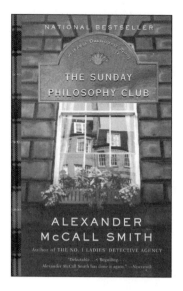

THE SUNDAY PHILOSOPHY CLUB

Author: *Alexander McCall Smith*

Publisher: Anchor Books, 2005

Web site: www.readinggroupcenter.com

Available in:
Paperback, 256 pages. $12.95
ISBN 1-4000-7709-5

Subject: Mystery/Detective (Fiction)

Summary: Introducing Isabel Dalhousie the heroine of the latest best-selling series from the author of *The No. 1 Ladies' Detective Agency.* Isabel, the editor of the *Review of Applied Ethics* and an occasional amateur sleuth, has been accused of getting involved in problems that are, quite frankly, none of her business. In this first installment, Isabel witnesses a man fall to his death. Against the advice of her no-nonsense housekeeper Grace and her romantically challenged niece Cat, she is morally bound to solve this case. Complete with wonderful Edinburgh atmosphere and characters straight out of a Robert Burns poem, *The Sunday Philosophy Club* is a delightful treat from one of our most beloved authors.

"Delectable. . . . Beguiling. . . . Alexander McCall Smith has done it again."—Newsweek

Alexander McCall Smith is the author of the huge international phenomenon, The No. 1 Ladies' Detective Agency series, and The Sunday Philosophy Club series. He was born in what is now known as Zimbabwe, and he was a law professor at the University of Botswana and at Edinburgh University. He lives in Scotland, where in his spare time he is a bassoonist in the RTO (Really Terrible Orchestra).

Topics for Discussion

1. Isabel Dalhousie is a single, wealthy, literary woman of settled habits with a strong interest in moral behavior. In what ways is she a model female sleuth, and in what ways is she a surprising one? How does she compare with other female detectives in literature?

2. Cat is annoyed at Isabel's tendency to get involved in things that are none of her business. Isabel insists, on the other hand, that the man who fell from the balcony entered her "moral space"—and that she therefore has a moral obligation to him. Is Isabel correct in arguing for proximity as a basis for moral claims?

3. Isabel raises the question of unequal desire in love when she reflects, "We do not like those who are completely available, who make themselves over to us entirely." Do you feel this accurately reflects Cat's emotional reaction to Jamie? Does this explain Isabel's continuing interest in John Liamor?

4. Why is the novel called *The Sunday Philosophy Club*, if the club seems to be purely notional, never having met? Are readers the members of this club, as if by reading the novel they are entering into Isabel's mind, which is constantly engaged in philosophical questioning?

5. It is Neil who comes to Isabel and tells her of Mark Fraser's knowledge of insider trading at his firm, thus turning the case into an investigation of a murder. How surprising is the ultimate revelation of how Mark died, and why? How is the crime's solution linked to the theme of truth and honesty?

6. The Edinburgh setting is a crucial element of *The Sunday Philosophy Club*. It is a city where respectability is highly valued, but, according to Isabel, is also built on hypocrisy. Is Isabel an exemplary product of Edinburgh's Protestant bourgeoisie, or not? What aspects of her life, or her character, place her in the position of outsider? Who in the text best represents traditional Scots respectability?

For a complete Reading Group Guide, to find about this and other books by Alexander McCall Smith, to sign up for his Fan Club, and more, visit www.alexandermccallsmith.com

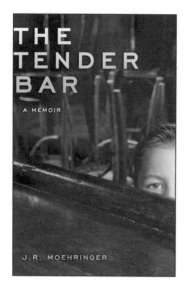

THE TENDER BAR
A Memoir

Author: *J.R. Moehringer*

Publisher: Hyperion Books, 2005

Website: www.TenderBar.com

Available in:
Hardcover, 384 pages. $23.95
ISBN 1-4013-0064-2

Subject: Memoir/Family Relationships/
Coming of Age (Nonfiction)

Summary: A moving, vividly told memoir full of heart, drama, and exquisite comic timing, about a boy striving to become a man, and his romance with a bar.

J.R. Moehringer grew up listening for a voice: It was the sound of his missing father, a disc jockey who disappeared before J.R. spoke his first words. As a boy, J.R. would press his ear to a clock radio, straining to hear in that resonant voice the secrets of masculinity, and the keys to his own identity. J.R.'s mother was his world, his anchor, but he needed something else, something he couldn't name. So he turned to the bar on the corner, a grand old New York saloon that was a sanctuary for all types of men—cops and poets, actors and lawyers, gamblers and stumblebums. The flamboyant characters along the bar taught J.R., tended him, and provided a kind of fatherhood by committee. Through it all, the bar offered shelter from failure, from rejection, and eventually from reality—until at last the bar turned J.R. away.

"The Tender Bar *will make you thirsty for that life—its camaraderie, its hilarity, its seductive, dangerous wisdom."* —**Richard Russo, author of** *Empire Falls*

". . . *the life of this young boy/man trying to find a place in the world resonated deeply with me."* —**Mitchell Kaplan, owner of Books and Books**

J.R. Moehringer, winner of the Pulitzer Prize for feature writing in 2000, is a national correspondent for the *Los Angeles Times* and a former Niemann Fellow at Harvard University. He lives in Denver, Colorado.

Topics for Discussion

1. J.R. has a difficult childhood, but there are also many positive elements. Compare Moehringer's portrait of childhood to other memoirs you've read.

2. There are various portrayals of "good" and "bad" men in the memoir. What are the different definitions of goodness in men?

3. In what ways is alcohol both a positive and a negative factor in the lives of the various characters?

4. Do you think J.R.'s mother's experiences are representative of the struggles of many single mothers? Do you think she is a strong character? Did you admire her, or empathize with her?

5. Did you find J.R.'s grandmother a sympathetic character? Did her dilemma feel familiar to you?

6. J.R.'s grandfather is cruel most of the time, but he has occasional moments of greatness, such as at J.R.'s school breakfast. What do you think motivated J.R.'s grandfather? Did you find him likable?

7. J.R. grows up without a present father. How do you think his search for a masculine identity compares to that of men who grew up with fathers—good or bad—which were more present in their lives?

8. The men along the bar are depicted warts and all—did you consider them positive role models? Which of the men was most appealing to you, and why?

9. J.R. notices that the men in the bar have conflicting attitudes toward success in other men. What does this stem from? Was it familiar to you?

10. Consider the importance of sports in men's lives and relationships with each other.

11. In what ways do characters and circumstances in *The Tender Bar* resemble that of *The Great Gatsby*, particularly with respect to class and aspiration?

12. In what ways was J.R.'s enormous ambition a positive element in his life, and in what ways was it the source of pain? Is this inevitable?

13. Did you find Sidney sympathetic?

14. How does the way the events of the epilogue tied together the themes of the memoir? Did you feel resolution? Did you think J.R. had changed?

15. Did you see yourself and any of your own experiences as a parent, child, man or woman in the memoir?

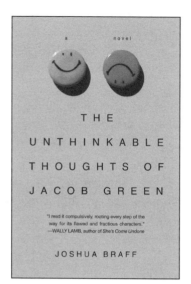

THE UNTHINKABLE THOUGHTS OF JACOB GREEN

Author: *Joshua Braff*

Publisher: Plume Books, 2005

Website: www.penguin.com

Available in:
Paperback, 272 pages. $14.00
ISBN 0-452-28670-0

Subject: Family Relationships/
Jewish Studies (Fiction)

Summary: Jacob Green doesn't mean to disappoint his father, but he can't help thinking the most unthinkable (and very funny) thoughts about public-school humiliation, Hebrew-school disinclination, and in-home sex education (with the live-in nanny!). If only his mother hadn't started college at thirty-six (and fallen for her psychology professor). If only he were more like his rebellious older brother (suspended from Hebrew school for drawing the rabbi in a threesome with a lobster and a pig). If only Jacob could confront his overbearing father and tell him he doesn't want to sing in synagogue, attend est classes, write the perfect thank-you note, or even live in the same house with Abram Green. But, of course, he can't. That would be unthinkable.

"A funny, heart-twisting story. . . . Braff deftly captures the monumental and miniscule moments of everyday life." —USA Today

Joshua Braff has an MFA in creative writing. He grew up in New Jersey and now lives with his wife and children in Oakland, California.

Topics for Discussion

1. In the book's first chapter, "Housewarming," the reader is introduced to the Green family (as are the Greens' party guests) and witnesses first-hand the awkward, tense, and sometimes inauthentic dynamic that exists between Abram Green and the members of his family. What was your initial reaction to Mr. Green's over-the-top display—or "Introduction"—of his sons, daughter, and wife? How does this first impression compare with your impression of him at the novel's conclusion? How does he develop—or avoid development—as a character/person?

2. In the chapter "Going Public," Jacob's learning disability is revealed not only to the reader, but also to Jacob himself. Discuss the significance of this discovery to Jacob, and how it affects his self-perception. Also discuss Abram Green's inability to reconcile Jacob's failures in school with his ability to read Hebrew, and the ways in which this affects his son.

3. Is Abram Green a sympathetic or likeable character in any way? Compare his obsessive, tyrannical hold over his family with the moments when he seems on the brink of begging for their approval and devotion.

4. Consider the "unthinkable thoughts" of Jacob Green, and how they affect the tone and pace of the book. Are they really as "unthinkable," or shocking, as he deems them to be? How do they work within the structure of the book—how do they interrupt, or help, the pace of the novel? Discuss the merit of the moments when his unthinkable thoughts are used to a humorous effect (i.e., in "The Sabbath") and the moments when they are used to convey more serious and poignant information (his mother's speech at the end of "Curtain").

5. Discuss Jacob's refusal to admit to his father's volatile and violent temper when Megan asks about it. Did Abram's behavior border on physical and emotional abuse? Was Megan right to refrain from contacting the authorities? Discuss the ways in which Jacob's accident was a direct or indirect consequence of the fight.

6. At the end of the novel, Jacob dresses for synagogue and then takes off running down the street. For the first time, the reader is outside of his unthinkable thoughts, and left wondering, like the bystanders he describes: "Where the hell is that kid going so fast? Where the hell is that kid going?" Evaluate the ending of the novel? Why is it important that we not know, conclusively, where he's going? Where do you imagine he *is* going?

For complete reading group guide, visit www.penguin.com.

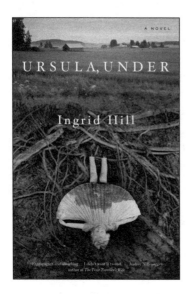

URSULA, UNDER

Author: *Ingrid Hill*

Publisher: Penguin, 2005

Website: www.penguin.com

Available in:
Paperback, 496 pages. $15.00
ISBN 0-14-303545-2

Subject: Identity (Fiction)

Summary: One of the most widely praised and rapturously entertaining first novels in recent years begins with a little girl falling down an abandoned mineshaft in Michigan's Upper Peninsula. Her name is Ursula Maki, she's part Chinese, part Finnish, only two years old, and soon the dangerous effort to rescue her has an entire country glued to the TV. As it follows that effort, *Ursula, Under* re-creates the chain of ancestors, across two thousand years, whose lives culminate in the fragile miracle of a little girl underground: a Chinese alchemist in the third century BC, the orphaned playmate to a seventeenth-century Swedish queen, the casualty of a mining accident that eerily foreshadows Ursula's, and many more. A work of symphonic richness and profound empathy, *Ursula, Under* dramatically demonstrates that no one is truly alone.

"Extravagant and absorbing . . . I didn't want it to end."
—Audrey Niffenegger, author of *The Time Traveler's Wife*

*"[Hill] astounds with her ability to meld simply and beautifully told stories, stories with an air of fable about them." —**The Washington Post Book World***

Ingrid Hill is the author of the short story collection Dixie Church Interstate Blues. She earned her Ph.D. in English from the University of Iowa and has twice received grants from the National Endowment for the Arts. She has twelve children, including two sets of twins. She lives in Iowa City.

Topics for Discussion

1. Although Ingrid Hill sets much of *Ursula, Under* in distant historical times, she writes almost all of the novel in the present tense. How might this choice affect the reader's response to her narrative?

2. Many of the figures in the historical chapters of *Ursula, Under* are potentially rich enough to be the heroes of their own separate novels. Which of these characters would be the best subject for a complete book, and why?

3. A sparkling scene takes place in "The Minister of Maps" when Ming Tao challenges Father Josserand to explain the mysteries of Christianity to her. Although the scene illustrates the depth of Josserand's humor and humanity, it also reveals his willingness to entertain blasphemous ideas. What are the most important questions raised about religion, and about Josserand's character, in this story?

4. *Ursula, Under* is a book laden with seemingly senseless catastrophes. Does Hill appear to find moral or cosmic significance in suffering? If so, what is that significance?

5. The sexual pairings and circumstances by which the bloodlines are carried forward in this novel often anything but conventional. There is a general scarcity of long, happy, monogamous unions. What does the unusual quality of the relationships contribute to Hill's novel?

6. Can *Ursula, Under* be classified as a feminist novel, and, if so, what are the features of Hill's idea of feminism?

7. Ingrid Hill comments repeatedly on the characters inability to remember the past and the impossibility of foreseeing the future. Why do you think she chose to place such powerful emphasis on states of not knowing?

8. In some ways, *Ursula, Under* can be thought of as a protracted response to Jinx Muehlenberg's question, "Why are they wasting all that money and energy on a goddamn half-breed trailer-trash kid?" How successfully does the novel respond to that question? Are the stories submerged in a person's hereditary past a persuasive reason for caring about that person? Are we truly willing to embrace the premise that every person is, as Hill says with reference to Ursula, "priceless . . . to the planet"?

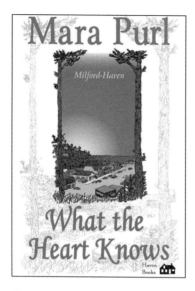

WHAT THE
HEART KNOWS
Milford-Haven—Book One

Author: *Mara Purl*

Publisher: Haven Books, 2005

Website: www.havenbooks.net

Available in:
Paperback, 160 pages. $12.95
ISBN 1-584360-01-1

Subject: Women's Fiction/Small-town Life/California Coastal (Fiction)

Summary: Artist Miranda Jones has escaped her privileged upbringing and is putting down roots in the picturesque coastal town of Milford-Haven. While busy painting in her studio, she receives a visit from Zack Calvin. Either he's a throwback to the wealthy men she's trying to outrun, or he's the man she's been dreaming about. On Main Street, Sally is dishing up home cooking in her restaurant and eavesdropping on everything that goes on in Milford-Haven. Environmental Planning Commissioner Samantha Hugo's personal journal reveals deep secrets from her past. Meanwhile, this peaceful town is unaware that reporter Chris Christian is being murdered while investigating a story.

"In Mara Purl's books the writing is crisp and clean, the dialogue realistic, the scenes well described. I salute her ingenuity." —**Bob Johnson, Former Managing Editor, The Associated Press**

"Mara Purl tells stories from the heart. Don't miss her Milford-Haven novels." —**Kathy (Mrs. Louis) L'Amour**

Mara Purl created Milford-Haven U.S.A., the first American radio drama broadcast by the BBC where it reached an audience of 4.5 million listeners throughout the U.K. For her creative and public service work, she was named one of twelve Women of the Year 2002 by the Los Angeles County Commission for Women. Her book of short stories, *Christmas Angels*, was named a 2005 Merit Book by the Colorado Independent Publishers Association. *What the Heart Knows* is her first novel, and the first in a twelve-book series that will comprise the Milford-Haven Novels.

Topics for Discussion

1. What are the dynamics of Milford-Haven? What is nurturing and supportive about a small town? When should privacy take a back seat to "public good"? Do you feel you have an absolute right to privacy?

2. Is Samantha in crisis? At what point have we encountered her in her life? Why does Samantha keep a journal? What function does journal writing perform in her life? Why do people keep journals? Have you ever kept a journal? What did it do for you?

3. Is Chris careful or foolhardy? Does she place her job or her personal life first? Was her trip to the Clarke house impetuous or well-calculated? Should a journalist do almost anything to get at the truth?

4. Would you agree Jack is a "head" person rather than a "heart" person? Do relationships make us more complete? Or do we first establish our completeness, then bring this quality to a relationship? Would you choose a life partner with your head, or with your heart?

5. Do you believe Miranda "makes" things happen when she paints intuitively? What makes an artist essentially different from other people? How do you explain synchronicity or coincidence in your life?

6. What are Zelda's motives? Do you think she's benevolent or malevolent? Why is Cynthia so calculating at such a young age? Why do some women manipulate every personal and business relationship? Do you think there are times coercion is justified? Have you sometimes used it in your own personal or professional life?

7. Is Miranda responding to a deep and soulful recognition when she meets Zack? Is she wise in pursuing a relationship with him, or is she treading on dangerous ground? How can you tell whether or not you've met the "right" person?

8. As a former journalist who wrote for the *Associated Press, The Financial Times of London, Rolling Stone, the Christian Science Monitor*, and the *Mainichi Daily News*, Mara Purl was trained to do extensive research and to report accurately. How might her journalistic background have influenced her as a novelist?

9. Why is this book called *What The Heart Knows*? Does this phrase apply only to Samantha and her journal writing? How might this apply to Miranda's meeting Zack? Does important information come to you through both head and heart?

When All Is Said And Done
A Novel By Robert Hill

WHEN ALL IS SAID AND DONE

Author: *Robert Hill*

Publisher: Graywolf Press, April 2006

Website: www.graywolfpress.org

Available in:
Hardcover, 180 pages. $20.00
ISBN 1-55597-442-2

Subject: Marriage/Parenting (Fiction)

Summary: In the early 1960s, Myrmy stubs her toe in the predawn hours on her way to soothe her infant son, cursing the latest nurse for not waking up, again. Dressed to the nines, it is Myrmy who is off to an executive position writing advertising copy for shampoo. Her husband, Dan, who fought in two wars, sell ties and cooks dinner. A Jewish couple living in an exclusive suburb of New York, Myrmy powers through her life in high heels and Dan silently suffers the mysterious aftereffects of a radiation experiment conducted by the military. Together they raise a family.

Robert Hill offers a distinctive and breathless portrayal of an ordinary and extraordinary marriage told through the alternating voices of husband and wife. *When All is Said and Done* is steeped in an era, but the anatomy of a marriage—comprised of humor, fear, love, and vulnerability—resonates through the ages.

"When All is Said and Done *is a fresh, high-velocity cry from the heart, showing that love is the rose and the thorn at once, and that Mr. Robert Hill has taken a running start into what they used to call the literary scene.*" —**Ron Carlson**

Robert Hill has been writing advertising copy for movies for over twenty years. Hill is interested in writing about the gray area of relationships between husbands and wives, lovers and friends. He hopes to explore best intentions that go awry, that take hold of the heart, grow stronger through the years, and become a living, breathing thing that's as much a part of a couple's day-to-day lives as children and pets. He believes that no "I love you" is without them. He lives in Portland, Oregon.

Topics for Discussion

1. In *When All is Said and Done*, the two main characters, Myrmy and Dan take turns narrating the story of their marriage. What would change if only Myrmy or only Dan (but not both) told their story? What is gained when two people tell the same story? If someone other than you or your spouse were to tell your story, what kinds of details would they miss? What would they be able to add?

2. Discuss the sacrifices that Myrmy and Dan make in order to build and maintain their marriage. Do you think their differences prevent them from being happy? How are the shortcomings of each compensated in other ways?

3. Discuss Myrmy's conversation with the real estate agent. Why does the agent decline to offer her services at first? How did Myrmy find the agent? How does the nature of the conversation change when the agent accidentally tells Myrmy about her problems with pregnancy?

4. Dan seems to suffer from a mysterious disease that affects his mental and physical health. What causes him to change from a physically fit Army man to an overweight tie salesman with a heart problem? Does Myrmy's high-powered job threaten him? Or is he suffering from something in his past?

5. This book takes place at a time when women were just beginning to be hired for high-powered positions. How does Myrmy's career affect her relationships with the women in her life? How does it affect her self image?

6. In families with two working parents, children usually spend a significant amount of time with childcare workers. How do Myrmy and Dan interact with their children? How does the role of their nanny add or detract from their role as parents? How do childcare workers take part in family life? Who ultimately makes choices for the children; the parents or the childcare? Does the active role played by childcare workers change the modern definition of a family?

7. There are times when Myrmy and Dan don't seem to know, or even like, the other person. Is it possible to truly ever "know" another person?

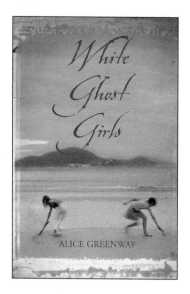

WHITE GHOST GIRLS

Author: *Alice Greenway*

Publisher: Black Cat, February 2006

Website: www.groveatlantic.com

Available in:
Paperback, 176 pages. $13.00
ISBN 0-8021-7018-8

Subject: Coming of Age/Sisters/
Family/Hong Kong/Vietnam War
(Fiction)

Summary: In Alice Greenway's exquisite gem of a novel, two girls tumble into their teenage years against the extraordinary backdrop of a Hong Kong dealing with the threat of communist China bubbling at its borders and the carnage in Vietnam that calls their father back time and again, like a moth to a flame. This astonishing literary debut is a tale of sacrifice and solidarity that gleams with the kind of intense, complicated love that only exists between sisters.

"White Ghost Girls *is so rich with detail and so charged with the colors and flavors of Hong Kong in the shadows of the Vietnam War that it's not only a great read, it's an olfactory experience. Alice Greenway captures the innocence of her young narrator with a voice that echoes with hard-earned wisdom, heartbreak, and love for a time and place.*"
—**Meghan Daum, author of** *The Quality of Life Report* **and** *My Misspent Youth*

Alice Greenway lived the itinerant life of a foreign correspondent's child. She grew up in Hong Kong, Bangkok, and Jerusalem, as well as in the United States. After graduating from Yale University in 1986, she returned to work in Hong Kong for two years. This is her first novel.

Topics for Discussion

1. In what ways does the narrator see herself and her sister as "castaways" and "secret sisters, shipwrecked sisters, and Vietcong sisters"?

2. How are Kate and Frankie different, physically and temperamentally? How do these differences influence their relationships with their parents?

3. "Hong Kong would be safer than Saigon; an old-fashioned British enclave, he called it. That was before the trouble started this summer." What is ironic about their parents' efforts to keep the girls safe from the horrors of Vietnam? Why are Kate and Frankie obsessed with war games and following the events in Vietnam?

4. What is the picture of the war in Vietnam as it emerges in the book?

5. How is Marianne, the mother, portrayed? Are there multiple facets in her daughters' perceptions of her? How does her art reflect her efforts to keep order and civility in her family's life?

6. The father, too, is a complex person. Is he a good father? Do you as a reader empathize with him as the book goes on?

7. What is the role of Ah Bing? As Amah is she an alternative mother figure for them? What kinds of worlds does she open?

8. How does Ah Bing's temple on Lantau Island compare to the English church, St. John's? What does the whole temple world mean to Ah Bing?

9. As Kate tries to understand her family and her world, is she a reliable narrator?

10. One of the big differences between Kate and Frankie is their attitude toward sex. Discuss this difference. What are Ah Bing's ideas on the subject?

11. Since the father is a photographer, is it odd that there are almost no photographs of his daughters? Why not?

12. On his rare trips home the father's bedtime stories as he lies on his back on the floor are of Mao, Ho Chi Minh and General Giap, Genghis Khan and Marco Polo. Is this his effort to share his world of journalism and storytelling?

13. How do you explain the last chapter, which stands as an epilogue written many years later? Is it Kate's epilogue only? "After all these years, this is all I want: a wooden stool, a bowl of rice, an army canteen, a secret comrade, the whooping cry of wild gibbons."

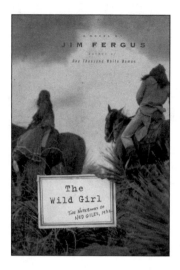

THE WILD GIRL
The Notebooks of Ned Giles, 1932

Author: *Jim Fergus*

Publisher: Hyperion Books, May 2006

Website: www.JimFergus.com

Available in:
Paperback, 368 pages. $14.95
ISBN 0-7868-8865-2
Hardcover, 355 pages. $23.95 (2005)
ISBN 1-4013-0054-5

Subject: Native Americans/Adventure/
Western/Mexico/Photography (Fiction)

Summary: When Ned Giles is orphaned as a teenager, he heads West hoping to leave his troubles behind. He joins the 1932 Great Apache Expedition on their search for a young boy, the son of a wealthy Mexican landowner, who was kidnapped by wild Apaches. But the expedition's goal is complicated when they encounter a wild Apache girl in a Mexican jail cell, victim of a Mexican massacre of her tribe that has left her orphaned and unwilling to eat or speak. As he and the expedition make their way through the rugged Sierra Madre mountains, Ned's growing feelings for the troubled girl soon force him to choose allegiances and make a decision that will haunt him forever.

In this novel based on historical fact, Jim Fergus takes readers on a journey of magnificent sweep and heartbreaking consequence peopled with unforgettable characters. With prose so vivid that the road dust practically rises off the page, *The Wild Girl* is an epic novel filled with drama, peril, and romance, told by a master.

"Poignant and spiritual. . . . Fergus' gift is in simple prose, vivid action and human stories." —Atlanta Journal-Constitution

"Enjoyably fast-paced and intelligently written, a vivid sketch of the early 20th-century West." —Rocky Mountain News

Jim Fergus is a freelance journalist whose writing appears in numerous publications. The author of two nonfiction books, his first novel, *One Thousand White Women*, remains a bestselling epic of the American West. He lives in southern Arizona.

Topics for Discussion

1. Is setting crucial to this story? How does Jim Fergus create the setting for us? What images or landscapes of the West and/or Mexico are most vivid in your mind?

2. This book is fiction based on historical fact. What did you learn about History from this book? What was familiar? Was the era—the 1930s —believable?

3. What do you think of Fergus' narrative framing device—starting and ending the tale in the present? What does it add to the story?

4. Name the different narrative voices in the book. Do you like the way the author jumps into different narrations? Does it work?

5. Charley is white, but is a respected member of the Apaches; the Huerta boy is Mexican but treated as an Apache child. What does it mean, then, to be an Apache? How does the "creed" of the Apaches transcend race? Can anyone become an Apache?

6. What do you think happened to Margaret after she sent the letter to Ned? In the end, did she achieve all she set out to do?

7. Does Jim Fergus write convincingly in the voice of female characters? How difficult it is as a writer to refrain from imposing your own experiences and thoughts through your characters?

8. Think of the men in positions of power: Chief Gatlin, Colonel Carrillo, Billy Flowers, Charley, and Indio Juan. What do they have in common? Which of the five is the best leader and why?

9. Mag and Tolley are both somewhat "outsiders" on the expedition. What unique challenges do they face? How do they individually deal with those challenges? Does Tolley change in the course of the story?

10. Ned's photograph of *La Nina Bronca* serves as a time capsule of sorts. Discuss this, and how art functions in the study of history.

11. Ned is able to separate himself from his camera, and as a result, his photographs tell their own version of the story. What in your life—a hobby, an artistic talent—allows you to do the same thing? Why is this important?

12. Did the author's note and the bibliography lead you to want to learn more about this period in Native American history? What about other historical novels? Do they inspire you to learn more about the real life characters?

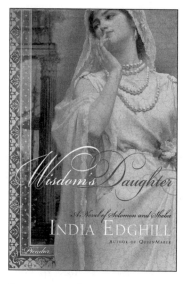

WISDOM'S DAUGHTER

Author: *India Edghill*

Publisher: Picador USA, 2005

Website: www.picadorusa.com

Available in:
Paperback, 432 pages. $14.00
ISBN 0-312-28940-5

Subject: Historical Fiction/Biblical/
Jewish Interest (Fiction)

Summary: Following *Queenmaker*, "her majestic debut" (*People* magazine), India Edghill's *Wisdom's Daughter* is a vivid and assiduously researched rendition of the Biblical tale of King Solomon and the Queen of Sheba. As the Queen's search for a true heir to her throne takes her to the court of the wisest man in the world, both she and the king learn how to value truth, love, and duty . . . and the king's daughter learns to be a forceful woman in a man's world. Told in a tapestry of voices that ring with authenticity, *Wisdom's Daughter* profoundly reveals the deep ties among women in a patriarchal world.

"Wisdom's Daughter *will appeal to the* Red Tent *crowd, both for its emphasis on the role of women in ancient Israel and for the author's ability to bring history to life. Edghill transforms a didactic fable, the story of King Solomon and his brief interaction with the Queen of Sheba, into a powerful love story. . . . Leisurely paced and focused on the wisdom of Solomon and the burdens of his reign, this atmospheric story is packed with political intrigue, illuminating the curious mixture of cultures and religions among the women of Solomon's court." —***Jennifer Baker, Booklist***

India Edghill is a librarian living in the mid-Hudson Valley, New York. She inherited her father's love of research and history. Edghill's favorite areas are the Ancient Near East, Victorian England, and India at any period.

Topics for Discussion

1. Who was Abishag, and why does she play such an integral part in the story? What was her relationship to King David, King Solomon, Queen Michal, and Princess Baalit?

2. What are the advantages of Sheba being a matriarchy? What are the disadvantages? How do they compare to those nations ruled by men?

3. What had the Israelites given up to gain a king? In exchange, what did the king bring them?

4. Why does Bilqis, the Queen of Sheba, hide her real reason in coming to King Solomon's court? How does her attitude towards Solomon change once she reveals her true purpose to him?

5. Why does Rehoboam hate Baalit? What does the incident of the cat reveal? What were his plans for Baalit when he eventually became king?

6. What was the significance of the ivory spindle? How did it reappear after being lost for so many years?

7. Who were Moonwind, Shams, and Uri? What did they represent to Baalit? How does Baalit endanger Uri?

8. Why did Baalit request the Lady Helike accompany her to Sheba? What was King Solomon's reaction to Baalit's request?

9. Will Baalit eventually marry Rahbarin? Why?

10. Why did Nikaulis turned back to remain with Benaiah? What were her plans thereafter?

11. What did King Solomon really learn from his foster mother, Queen Michal? What did Baalit really learn from her father, King Solomon?

12. The author says that Queen Michal forged King Solomon into a king who was "human fire and royal ice." Which other characters fit that description?

13. The narrative says, "Love, honor, duty—even wisdom, in the end, must yield to that." Which characters yielded to "love, honor, and duty"? Which characters did not?

14. Baalit says, ". . . all women and men are different—and they are all the same. Some would be happy anywhere, and some happy nowhere." Do you think this is true? What lessons are there in this book for women today?

The WITCH of COLOGNE

TOBSHA LEARNER

THE WITCH OF COLOGNE

Author: *Tobsha Learner*

Publisher: Forge, 2005
(Tom Doherty Associates, LLC)

Website: www.tor.com/forge

Available in:
Paperback, 480 pages. $14.95
ISBN 0-765-31430-4

Subject: Religion (Fiction)

Summary: In Tobsha Learner's *The Witch of Cologne*, 17th century heroine Ruth bas Elazer Saul is first introduced to the Zohar by her mother, and then by her nurse, Rosa, after her mother's passing. Ruth employs this sacred knowledge in her career as a midwife, using revolutionary methods of childbirth and healing that lead to accusations of witchcraft, imprisonment, and a forbidden love affair with Detlef Von Tennen: a Catholic vice-bishop of the Dome.

Set in the medieval cities of Cologne and Amsterdam during the time of the Inquisition, *The Witch of Cologne* is the story of the complex relationship between German Jewry and their Christian neighbors. It contains a fascinating mix of fictional and actual characters, such as humanist philosopher Benedict Spinoza, and an exploration of many of their philosophical notions. *The Witch of Cologne* examines the nature of love and personal beliefs, as well as the political, religious and social ideas of the time, inspiring pause for reflection today.

"In the tradition of books about strong Jewish women, including The Red Tent *and* Sarah . . . *this is the kind of all-consuming novel that readers hate to see end."*—***Booklist***

Tobsha Learner was born and raised in England and now divides her time among the US, the UK, and Australia. She is a renowned playwright and short story writer and has written for television and film in Australia and the US. Her collection of erotic short fiction, *Quiver*, has sold more than 150,000 copies around the world. The *Witch of Cologne* is her first historical novel.

Topics for Discussion

1. What was the prevalence of Kabbalah in 17th century midwifery?

2. In 2004, France banned students from wearing religious symbols such as headscarves, yarmulkes, and large crosses in public schools. What parallels can be drawn between this action and the restrictions imposed on the Jewish community in Germany in the 1660s and the 1930s?

3. Many people believe in ancient superstitions. "Touching wood" wards off evil and spilling salt is unlucky. Some use talismans or light candles to protect themselves or their families. How can these beliefs co-exist with a scientific view of the universe?

4. *The Witch of Cologne* is set during the early years of what came to be known as the Age of Enlightenment. However, this was also a time of superstition and hypocrisy. How does this tension play out in the novel?

5. Ruth bas Elazar Saul has been described as "a woman before her time" and "a potent mix of the old and the new." How does her character explore these ideas?

6. What kind of power was available to women in the 17th century? Discuss how Ruth uses power within and outside the system of her time and faith.

7. During the dawn of the Age of Enlightenment, the relative values of religion and science were shifting within European culture. Some suggest that the beginning of the Twenty-First Century is seeing another significant alteration in the roles of science and religion. Do you agree or disagree? What events might indicate that such a shift is taking place?

8. *The Witch of Cologne* is written in the present tense. Does the choice of tense affect the relationship between the reader and the text?

9. Religious law prohibits Jewish men from bearing arms. How did this affect relationships between the Jewish community and the larger world during the time of *The Witch of Cologne*? Do you think this restriction generated the sometimes widely-held belief that Jews were cowards? Did this restriction affect Jewish response to attacks in the Twentieth Century, like the pogroms in Russia or the Holocaust? When should people ignore a religious proscription?

Next on your list? Award-winning fiction for your Reading Group!

CIPA Merit Book 2005 *Honorable Mention* *Spiritual/Inspirational*	**IPPY Award 2001** *Finalist* *Multicultural Fiction*

### *Christmas Angels* ### *by Mara Purl*	### *Girl-On-Fire* ### *by Vicki Hessel Werkley*
Inspiring short stories from the acclaimed author of the Milford-Haven Novels	Powerful fiction based on a dynamic chapter of American history *An Adult Book also Recommended for Teens*

### *It's Christmas in Milford-Haven...*  *and each character has a dilemma perhaps only an "angel" can solve. Meet the beloved residents of the quaint little town on California's gorgeous Central Coast, where Christmas may never come at all, unless people listen to their Christmas Angels*	### *Abducted! How will she survive?* As the Red River War of 1874 rages across the plains of Texas and present-day Oklahoma, sixteen-year-old Carrie McEdan is home alone, yearning for a life beyond her realm of Victorian restrictions and household drudgery. Only moments later, she's forced from that soddy home and swept away into Comanche tribal life. Does she have the strength to endure? Can she find acceptance in this alien culture—perhaps even love and spiritual connection?

"Mara Purl's mix of a soap-opera format is a smash hit in Britain." *– the Los Angeles Times* "In Mara Purl's books, the writing is crisp and clean, the dialogue realistic, the scenes well described. I salute her ingenuity." *– Bob Johnson, Former Managing Editor, the Associated Press* "Mara Purl's story is beautifully told, with exquisite detail and gripping scenes that take you into the lives of these characters in a suspenseful and riveting way." *– Sam Summerlin New York Times Books Syndicate* "Mara Purl has captured our gentle yearning for a sweeter holiday season." *– Kathe Tanner, The Cambrian* "Mara Purl tells stories from the heart. Don't miss her Milford-Haven series!" *– Kathy (Mrs. Louis) L'Amour*	"The strength of this book is in the rich details of Native American culture in the 1870s. The smell of wood smoke and simmering stews; the 'tidy efficiency' of a tepee with its inner drape, rawhide trunks, and willow-slat beds; and the sounds of language and songs all encourage readers to experience the human complexities of tribal life. Even teens reluctantly fulfilling a dreaded historical fiction assignment should become caught up in the protagonist's bittersweet adventure with a people who will soon face many tragic losses of their own." *— School Library Journal* "Girl-On-Fire is a superbly written book... extraordinarily accurate about the daily life and responsibilities of Comanche women and with the Comanche language appropriately used. Vicki Werkley has done an outstanding job in her research of the Comanche People. I give this book two thumbs up!" *— Thekwane (Jolene Jimenez), Comanche Tribal Princess, 1988*

Read excerpts, find other books and discover more topics for discussion at our web site!

 www.havenbooks.net

$\mathcal{V}$OICES OF THE $\mathcal{S}$OUTH
(Re)Discover These Recently Published Novels

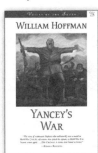
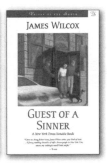

Malaise
A Novel
NANCY LEMANN

"Wryly funny, hilariously depraved, and filled with slashing observations about the cultures of the southern United States and southern California."*—Memphis Commercial Appeal*
$17.95 PAPER

Buffalo
A Novel
SYDNEY BLAIR

"Blair can be funny and stingingly precise about the destructive little boys often inhabiting grown men. A beauty of a first novel."*—Village Voice*
Online reading group guide available!
$17.95 PAPER

Yancey's War
A Novel
WILLIAM HOFFMAN

"The life of enlisted men in camp and on leave and the politics of the officer caste are reported in detail, with hilarity at times, as well as with sympathy."*—Library Journal*
$21.95 PAPER

Two from **JAMES WILCOX!**

"Wilcox has real comic genius. He is a writer to make us all feel hopeful."
—Anne Tyler, *New York Times Book Review*

Modern Baptists
A Novel
$18.95 PAPER

Guest of a Sinner
A Novel
$17.95 PAPER

In the Wink of an Eye
A Novel
KELLY CHERRY

"Outrageous characters are brought to life in a fast-paced tale that is fun to read."
—Houston Chronicle
$18.95 PAPER

Surfaces of a Diamond
A Novel
LOUIS D. RUBIN, JR.

"Charleston in the late 1930s . . . proves a baffling, traumatic, enriching time in a boy's life, and the reader shares it acutely."
—Booklist
$17.95 PAPER

LOUISIANA STATE UNIVERSITY PRESS
(800) 861-3477 • Visit **www.lsu.edu/lsupress** to learn more about all Voices of the South titles!

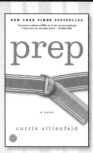

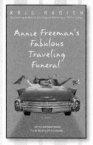
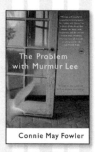

Book some quality time with the
best books available for reading groups:

Join the Reader's Circle

If you love reading and discussing
good books by some of the finest
authors in print, join the Reader's
Circle—and receive a FREE
Reader's Circle catalog, plus our
monthly e-newsletter.

For details go to:
www.thereaderscircle.com/register

WE ARE YOUR
ULTIMATE RESOURCE:

- More than 290 fiction and nonfiction
  selections by a host of remarkable writers
- Information on starting and running a
  reading group
- Novel ideas for reading group activities
- Tips on book selection and setting up
  phone chats with authors
- Ideas for booksellers and librarians
- A complete title index

STAY IN TOUCH AND
INFORMED ONLINE:

- Sneak-peek excerpts from the newest titles
- Recommendations for up-and-coming "must reads"
- Exclusive interviews with your favorite authors
- Opportunities for authors to visit your next book club meeting
- Special offers and promotions for advance reader's editions, author
  interviews on CD, and much more.

Go to www.thereaderscircle.com/register and register
to receive your FREE Reader's Circle catalog &
monthly e-newsletter.

Read the Classics

The Annotated Shakespeare series provides today's readers with immediate access to the tools they need to better comprehend these great works. Each volume includes an informative introduction by the distinguished scholar Burton Raffel, a critical essay by Harold Bloom, and comprehensive on-page annotations that assist with vocabulary, pronunciation, prosody, and alternative readings of phrases and lines. Handsome and affordable ($6.95 each), these **paperback** editions invite every reader to get to know—or to become reacquainted with—the genius of Shakespeare.

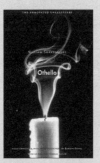

Othello

A Midsummer Night's Dream

The Taming of the Shrew

Romeo and Juliet

Macbeth

Hamlet

For sample scenes and selections from the Introductions, visit our website.

 YALE University Press • yalebooks.com

RESOURCES

THE INTERNET

Reading Group Choices Online—guides available from major publishers and independent presses that can be printed directly from the site: **ReadingGroupChoices.com**

For new book information, reading lists, book news and literary events, visit **ReadingGroupGuides.com, generousbooks.com, BookSpot.com, BookMuse.com, and BookReporter.com**. Looking for reading guides for children? Visit **KidsReads.com**.

For a complete guide to book clubs and reading groups with an outstanding collection of links and information for readers, visit **Book-Clubs-Resource.com.**

Interested in signed copies of books? Interested in meeting authors? Interested in learning about new books? Visit **booksignings.net.**

If you love classic books, and want to discuss them with like-minded people, visit **classicbookclub.co.uk.com.**

Publisher Web Sites — Find additional topics for discussion, special offers for book groups, and other titles of interest.

Algonquin Books of Chapel Hill—*algonquin.com*
Anchor Books—*readinggroupcenter.com*
Ballantine Books—*ballantinebooks.com/BRC*
Berkley Books—*penguin.com*
Calliope Press—*calliopepress.com*
Emmis Books—*emmisbooks.com*
Forge Books—*tor.com*
Graywolf Press—*graywolfpress.org*
Grove/Atlantic—*groveatlantic.com*
HarperCollins—*harpercollins.com*
Haven Books—*havenbooks.net*
HCI Books—*hcibooks.com*
Henry Holt & Company—*henryholt.com*
Hyperion Books—*hyperionbooks.com*

John Wiley & Sons - *wiley.com*
Louisiana State University Press—*lsu.edu*
MacAdam/Cage—*macadamcage.com*
Middleway Press—*middlewaypress.org*
MIRA Books—*mirabooks.com*
Penguin/Putnam Group—*penguin.com*
Picador USA—*picadorusa.com*
Plume Books—*penguin.com*
Random House—*randomhouse.com*
Red Wheel/Weiser/Conari Press—*redwheelweiser.com*
Riverhead Books—*penguin.com*
Roots West Press—*rochlin-roots.west.com*
Soft Skull Press—*softskull.com*
Thomas Dunne Books—*stmartins.com*
Unbridled Books—*unbridledbooks.com*
Vintage Books—*readinggroupcenter.com*
W.W. Norton—*wwnorton.com*
Yale University Press—*yalebooks.com*

NEWSLETTERS AND BOOK LISTS

BookWomen: A Readers' Community for Those Who Love Women's Words, a bimonthly "bookletter" published by the Minnesota Women's Press. Includes recommendations, news about the book world, and articles for and about women readers and writers.

> Subscription: $24/yr. (6 issues).
> Contact: book@womenspress.com
> Minnesota Women's Press
> 771 Raymond Ave., St. Paul, MN 55114
> (651) 646-3968
> Womenspress.com

Reverberations News Journal, Rachel Jacobsohn's publication of the Association of Book Group Readers and Leaders.

> Annual membership including subscription is $20.
> Contact: rachelj1@comcast.net
> P.O. Box 885 Highland Park, IL 60035.

BOOKS AND JOURNALS

Bibliotherapy: The Girl's Guide to Books for Every Phase of Our Lives by Nancy Peske and Beverly West. Published by DTP, ISBN 0-4405-0897-5, $14.95.

Book Lust: Recommended Reading for Every Mood, Moment, and Reason by Nancy Pearl. Published by Sasquatch Books, ISBN 1-57061-381-8, $16.95

More Book Lust: Recommended Reading for Every Mood, Moment, and Reason by Nancy Pearl, Published by Sasquatch Books, ISBN 1-57061-435-0, $16.95.

The Book Club Cookbook: Recipes and Food for Thought from Your Book Club's Favorite Books and Authors by Judy Gelman and Vicki Levy Krupp. Published by Tarcher/Penguin, ISBN 1-58542-322-X, $15.95.

The Book Group Book: A Thoughtful Guide to Forming and Enjoying a Stimulating Book Discussion Group. Edited by Ellen Slezak and Margaret Eleanor Atwood. Published by Chicago Review Press, ISBN 1-5565-2412-9, $14.95.

Circles of Sisterhood: A Book Discussion Group Guide for Women of Color by Pat Neblett. Published by Writers & Readers, ISBN 0-8631-6245-2, $14.

Contemporary Multi-Ethnic Novels by Women Coming of Age Together in the New America by Rochelle Holt, Ph.D. Published by Thanks Be to Grandmother Winifred Foundation, $5 + SASE (6" by 8"). Write to: 15223 Coral Isle Ct., Ft. Myers, FL 33919.

Family Book Sharing Groups: Start One in Your Neighborhood! By Marjorie R. Simic with Eleanor C. MacFarlane. Published by the Family Literacy Center, ISBN 1-8837-9011-5, $6.95.

Leave Me Alone, I'm Reading: Finding and Losing Myself in Books by Maureen Corrigan. Published by Random House, ISBN 0-375-50425-7, $24.95.

Literature Circles: Voice and Choice in Book Clubs and Reading Groups by Harvey Daniels. Published by Stenhouse Publishers, ISBN 1-5711-0333-3, $22.50.

Minnesota Women's Press Great Books. An annotated listing of 236 books by women authors chosen by over 3,000 women participating in Minnesota Women's Press Book Groups in the past 13 years. $10.95 + $2 s/h. (612) 646-3968.

The Mother-Daughter Book Club: How Ten Busy Mothers and Daughters Came Together to Talk, Laugh and Learn Through Their Love of Reading by Shireen Dodson and Teresa Barker. Published by HarperCollins, ISBN 0-0609-5242-3, $14.

The Readers' Choice: 200 Book Club Favorites by Victoria McMains. Published by Wm. Morrow, ISBN 0-6881-7435-3, $14.

The Reading Group Handbook: Everything You Need to Know to Start Your Own Book Club by Rachel Jacobsohn. Published by Hyperion, ISBN 0-786-88324-3, $12.95.

The Reading List: Contemporary Fiction, A Critical Guide to the Complete Works of 125 Authors. Edited by David Rubel. Published by Owl Books, ISBN 0-805055-27-4, $17.

Reading to Heal: A Reading Group Strategy for Better Health by Diane Dawber. Published by Quarry Press, ISBN 1-5508-2229-2, $9.95.

Talking About Books: Literature Discussion Groups in K-8 Classrooms by Kathy Short. Published by Heinemann, ISBN 0-3250-0073-5, $24.

Thirteen Ways of Looking at the Novel by Jane Smiley. Published by Knopf, ISBN 1-4000-4059-0, $26.95.

What to Read: The Essential Guide for Reading Group Members and Other Book Lovers (Revised) by Mickey Pearlman. Published by HarperCollins, ISBN 0-0609-5313-6, $14.

A Year of Reading: A Month-By-Month Guide to Classics and Crowd-Pleasers for You or Your Book Group by H. E. Ellington and Jane Freimiller. Published by Sourcebooks, ISBN 1-5707-1935-7, $14.95.

BOOK GROUP FAVORITES FROM 2004

Early in 2005, we asked book groups on *Reading Group Choices* Online to tell us about the books they read and discussed during the previous year that they enjoyed most. It's always interesting to see the hundreds of titles that get recommended—and which ones appear in the top 15.

BOOK GROUP FAVORITES FROM 2004

1. *The Secret Life* of Bees by Sue Monk Kidd (Viking)
2. *The Da Vinci Code* by Dan Brown (Doubleday)
3. *Life of Pi* by Yann Martel (Harcourt)
4. *The Kite Runner* by Khaled Hosseini (Riverhead)
5. *Middlesex* by Jeffrey Eugenides (Picador USA)
6. *Angry Housewives Eating Bon Bons* by Lorna Landvik (Ballantine)
7. *Bel Canto* by Ann Patchett (HarperCollins)
8. *The Five People You Meet in Heaven* by Mitch Albom (Hyperion)
9. *The Red Tent* by Anita Diamant (Picador USA)
10. *The Curious Incident of the Dog in the Night Time* by Mark Haddon (Vintage)
11. *East of Eden* by John Steinbeck (Penguin Books)
12. *The Time Travelers Wife* by Audrey Niffenegger (Harvest/HBJ Book)
13. *Girl With a Pearl Earring* by Tracy Chevalier (Plume)
14. *#1 Ladies Detective Agency* by Alexander McCall Smith (Anchor)
15. *A Fine Balance* by Rohinton Mistry (Vintage)

INDEX BY SUBJECT/INTEREST AREA